Horse Feather Farm

Horse Feather Farm

A Journey of a Lifetime

Marcia Cromie

Foreword by TJ Martini

Second Printing
December 2023

ISBN 978-1-7321457-0-2
(International Trade Paper Edition)

Editor
TJ Martini

Layout and Design
Gary Lebeck

Front Cover Art
DeAnn Foster

Back Cover Photograph
Gary Lebeck

Publisher
Rivertree Media

Printed in the United States of America
27 26 25 24 23 / RMG / 10 9 8 7 6 5 4 3 2

Dedication

I proudly and humbly dedicate this book to all those who walked this journey with me—my family, my friends, my loved ones, and every child, horse and animal that passed through our gates at Horse Feather Farm.

And to God who made it all possible.

Table of Contents

Memories

Acknowledgements

With special thanks:
To my Savior Jesus Christ; my strength and my provider.

To my husband Dick; for your love, prayers, patience and great sense of humor.

To Toni Martini; my beloved friend, confidant and editor.

To Gary Lebeck; for sharing your talents and knowledge to get this book laid out and published.

To Jack Foster; the brother I never had, who accepted me and mentored me with kindness, knowledge and love.

To Jessica Altmayer; a sister in so many ways; you taught me all I needed to know with love and understanding.

To my soul sister and great encourager DeAnn Foster; for your creative energy, for designing the Horse Feather Farm logo and your cover art for this book... and so much more.

To my friend and supporter Jayne Fletcher; for creating Horse Feather Farm business cards and materials, and for many other ideas for success.

To my dear friend Kash Grimes; you knew how much I didn't know and took me under your wing, and taught me.

To my sidekick, Linda Bartelt; I could have never done the last few years of camp without you and your family.

To Daniel Cruz; you are my forever faithful friend and helper and secretly the head of "buildings and grounds" at Horse Feather Farm.

And for every volunteer; who came through the gates at Horse Feather Farm; my dependence on you was immense, and you never once let me down.

Foreword

For the past 20 years, God has given me a heart to spread His glory by writing true stories that come from ordinary people all over the world. It has been my greatest joy helping these individuals share what they have been through, and then watching as God turns the ordinary into extraordinary. Yet few testimonies have touched me more than this one.

The story you are about to read is true. It may even be life-changing as it has been for so many others who have crossed the path of this amazing woman. As you turn each page, you will understand why her story is such a gift from God.

I haven't known Marcia Cromie very long, at least not when compared to the others she had befriended over the past several decades. I met Marcia about five years ago, at our women's Bible Study Fellowship (BSF) when she was assigned to our class. She had joined our group late in the year because she and her husband Dick had recently moved to the area from Southern California, and our class had already started. I'll never forget that day:

Marcia had come in late (which, if you know Marcia, you know this is not unusual), and she sat down next to me. Prior to Marcia joining us, whenever our leader would ask a question from the homework, there always seemed to be a short, uncomfortable silence. However, once Marcia came, there was silence no more!

As I listened every week, I began forming an opinion about this woman and soon realized how much I admired her boldness as she gave each heartfelt answer. Marcia didn't know a soul, and yet she seemed so brave to me, sharing and responding in depth to each question. Me? I would have never been so bold as to respond in a room where no one knew me, but it didn't stop Marcia. However, her being the stranger—the new kid on the block—did not last long, for she soon worked her way into all of our hearts.

Today, Marcia and I spend a great deal of time together, not only at BSF, but also at each other's houses with some of our other close BSF friends. In fact, every so often, we even allow our husbands to tag along.

We girls (Diana, Liz, Karen, Alexis, Marcia and me) have formed a bond like no other in such a short time...praying, loving, laughing and many times even crying together. We refer to ourselves as the COL—Circle of Love; and that we are!

As I read through Marcia's story and helped to put it together, I began to admire my friend even more. To think of how many young, impressionable lives this woman has touched over the years is a force to be reckoned with.

I did not grow up in a godly family, nor did my family attend church on a regular basis. I also never knew what I wanted to do at such a young age. But Marcia did. It may have taken her 45 years to get there, but the desires of her heart never went away. She wanted a horse and she truly believed that someday God would provide, and that she would use this blessing to bring Him glory. And that she has done! Oh, to have had that kind of faith and determination. God's plan had fallen right into her lap.

While I was reading all the loving comments in the back of this book, from kids all over the world who had once been part of Horse Feather Farm, it occurred to me that had I been blessed as a child to have had a "Marcia" in my life, I probably wouldn't have made the mistakes I made or chosen so poorly, which would have made life so much easier for me.

Marcia had a unique way of letting these kids know what was right and what wasn't, and she did it with genuine kindness, love and humor bringing God into every situation, and then taking that situation and making it a lesson which she would teach to the young lives that were in her care. She constantly challenged these kids to be respectful, kinder and more understanding, and when their time at HFF was over, they all left a much better person than when they first arrived.

Every child that passed through the gates at HFF learned something. Every child grew into someone more than they would have been. Every child took with them a life's lesson they could share—all because of Marcia's guidance. What a joy it is for me to be a part of her story; I feel blessed to love her and honored to call her my friend.

TJ Marteni

Founder, Bathed in His Glory Encouragement Cards
and Christian author

Introduction

"If you want to change the world, pick up your pen and write." Martin Luther (1483-1586)

This is my story, my love letter to God. One of the reasons for me writing my story is so I can look back on my life and see how God's hands have always been present, how He continues to lead me, how He calls and nurtures me, disciplines and grows me, but most of all, how He loves me.

The places I've lived and the people who have come into my life over the years have all played a special role in who I am today. And, of course, every horse and pony that has been in my care from the time I was 12 years old came straight from Heaven's gate. Without all of them, I would not be the person I am today. God knew all along who and what I would need, and He hand-delivered each one of them to me.

As I look into life's rearview mirror, I can see all those that God purposely placed in my path to help guide and steady me when I could not find my way. Those times when I fell or veered off course, God was always there to bring someone or something into my life, to pick me up, and to rescue me. Even those who may not have been Christians (or even human for that matter), God still used them to help mold me into what He wanted me to be in order for me to fulfill His plan and purpose on this earth.

It is my heartfelt belief that God has a plan and purpose for each one of us. I am living proof that He can and will use anyone, at any time, to fulfill His will. I am more humble than I can say and so very grateful to be His daughter and to be used in such a way as this—my story is for His glory alone.

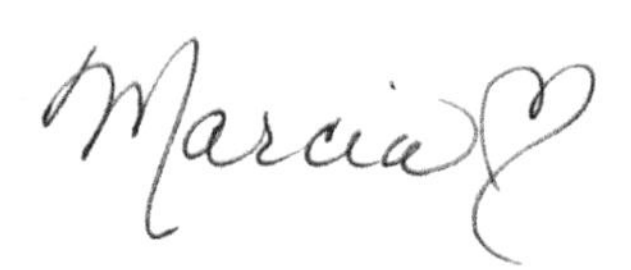

CHAPTER 1

Desires of the Heart

From the time I can remember, I have always loved horses. When I was very young, I started collecting them. Not the real ones, of course, but the stuffed, plastic or porcelain ones—big or small, however they came. If it resembled a horse, I brought it home and added it to my ever-growing collection. By the time I was thinking about college, I had over a hundred of these animals in my possession spread out all over my bedroom. But when I actually went off to college, I had to leave them behind. To my dismay, shortly after I left, my mom sold them all at a garage sale, which is still a sore spot for me to write about or even remember.

My mom and dad had four daughters. I was their second and was born when my parents were living in San Francisco. My three other sisters were all born in Pasadena (which might explain a lot). Mollie was the oldest. Then there was me (Marcia), Georgia, and baby Nancy. We were all about 3½ years apart. I'm sure my mom planned it that way for college—one out, the next one in! I remember one year Mollie graduating college, me graduating high school, Georgia graduating junior high, and Nancy from elementary school. My mother—always a planner and organizer.

Mollie was the typical high achiever in school, Marcia was not. Georgia was the sweetest and most obedient. Nancy, being shy, just hung on at the end of the group. She didn't talk until she was around five—she didn't have to. She would point, and we would get it for her.

When I was ten, my father accepted a job in Massachusetts and our family moved to the quaint little town of Andover. At the time, Andover was still a small "rural" town about 20 minutes north of Boston. There were numerous working farms still running successfully—dairy, poultry, and vegetable—and were scattered around the outskirts of town. Like most of the towns in New England, Andover had a main street which went straight through the downtown area. It was logically called Main Street.

Before moving to Massachusetts, I had attended school in California—grades Kindergarten through the 4th grade—but I had always struggled with my lessons and had a hard time with comprehension. An "A" student I was not! So it was decided that when we moved to Andover, I would repeat the 4th grade in the fall. My mom had convinced me that I had the perfect opportunity for this 4th grade "do over" and no one would be the wiser, because no one would know it was a "do-over", except me. However, the blabbermouth that I was known to be could not keep a secret, and I told everyone! One would typically not brag about this, but then again, I was not the norm. What was I thinking?

After a time, we all settled in nicely to the New England way of life. Well, maybe not so much my mother. It took her a while. She was a California girl through and through, and I think she almost had a heart attack when we had our first snowstorm. It came down hard, it was white, and it was everywhere. My sisters and I loved it though, especially the "snow days" when we didn't have to go to school. On those days, we would take full advantage of the weather.

There was this piece of property two streets up from us that was owned by Phillips Academy (All Boys Prep School), and on the property was a small body of water called Rabbits Pond. In the summer we would fish for hornpout, and in the winter we would all go ice skating. We spent many a snow day there, too.

The house my parents purchased in Andover was a big, beautiful Victorian structure, built before the turn of the century. To a ten-year-old, this house was huge. It was three full floors including a large finished basement—seven bedrooms, four full baths, and a large country-style kitchen with an eating area that had bench seating like a restaurant.

The house was built around 1889. Even though there were plenty of rooms to choose from, my sister Georgia and I decided to be in the same room together—no one wanted to be up on the 3rd floor alone. We also discovered many hiding places for us girls. The four of us had great imaginations as we made up stories about monsters living in these hiding places and then coming to life at our command. Oh, what fun we had together. When I got into high school, I eventually moved up to the 3rd floor so I could be away from all my sisters—you know, I needed to be independent—my own space. This was the 60's.

The house was so big that my mom had to yell to get our attention. I think she was a screamer by nature anyway. We also had a fire alarm throughout the house with each room having a little red button over the door threshold. At one point, we even had numbers assigned to us when she wanted us to come. If Mom pressed the button one time, it would buzz, and that was for Mollie. I was two buzzers, Georgia was three, and Nancy was four. Dad didn't have a buzzer number. He didn't need one, nor did he want one.

As I mentioned, I am the second of four girls. My older sister Mollie, who studied psychology in college, used to always tell me that I was a typical "second child". Whatever that meant! She learned more about this "syndrome" in college, and there seemed to be something to it. Well, at least in our family there did.

I had some learning disabilities (no doubt one of the reasons I was held back in the 4th grade)—Dyslexia they called it, though more is known about it today than it was back then. I was never a good student because of this disability, and I struggled greatly throughout my entire school career. My family learned to praise God whenever Marcia brought home a "B".

My parents tried their best to always encourage me, but I knew I frustrated them. I frustrated myself, too! I also learned that I had what they call today ADHD (Attention-Deficit/Hyperactivity Disorder), although no one knew anything about this disorder back then. I couldn't sit still. I had to keep moving. I remember asking my mom once when I was an adult, "What did you do with me?" She said,

"I just kept you busy." And that she did—piano lessons, tennis lessons, church youth group, dance lessons, ice skating lessons—whatever she could put me in to keep me busy and moving.

My mother was interested in all four of us girls being exposed to music and to take music lessons, mainly piano. I remember (what seemed like once a month, but probably more like once a quarter) we would travel by train or by car into Boston to spend an afternoon at the Boston Symphony. First, we'd have lunch, and then we would attend the symphony. I liked the lunch part, but I thought the symphony was kind of boring, except for the conductor, Arthur Fiedler, who I thought was great. I truly believe the experience I received from these outings is why I love to listen to classical music today. Guess my mom knew something, huh?

Then there were the piano lessons. We all had some musical abilities, but Georgia had the most talent. Mollie and Nancy either faked it or didn't have the talent, so after a while mom let them drop out. I ended up taking lessons for 11 years. I had two teachers die on me—that in itself should have told my mom something! I probably killed them!

I practiced 45 minutes a day, and several times I had

to have someone (i.e. my mom) standing behind me so I wouldn't mess around. Not surprisingly, Georgia, being the obedient one, would actually go to the piano and practice without being told. She went on to major in music and has taught music for more than 35 years.

My final recital was at the Methuen Organ Hall which, at the time, housed the 3rd largest organ in the world. I was the last one listed on the program. I walked out onto this huge stage feeling brave and confident, then sat down and played Rachmaninoff Prelude in C# Minor. I can't even play two lines with two hands now—forget the whole piece. After that, I never played again. But what the piano gave me was the basis for music and allowed me to teach myself how to play the guitar.

Music was a healthy distraction, yet I still desperately wanted a horse, and every birthday and Christmas I would ask for one. It was always at the top of my list. I knew I didn't stand much of a chance for my wish to come true (not only because there was no place to keep it, but because there were three other girls in our family and it wouldn't have been fair to my sisters). But still, I asked.

This one birthday, however, when I was in the 5th grade, I thought for sure my parents had given in. My birthday is in November, and it's the loveliest time in New England with all the falling leaves and cold crisp air. My parents had bought me something in advance and even gave me a few hints, which was a first. They told me I would be receiving something "very large and brown". My stomach dropped. Could it be? Dare I hope? "Oh please, God, please!" I cried out.

During school, I found myself daydreaming about the possibility of a horse of my own. My very own! I never paid too much attention in class anyway, so daydreaming gave me somewhere to go in my mind. And oh, did I dream! I could actually see this horse and feel it under me as we rode off into the fields. Large? Brown? What else could it be?

When my birthday finally arrived, I ran all the way home from school. I was so excited I could barely catch my breath. But I didn't see a horse anywhere, in the front or the back. Then I went inside, and my mom told me that my "big, brown" present was in my room. I was confused. How could this be? A horse ...in my room? My hopes began to dwindle.

I turned quickly, then ran up the stairs and opened my bedroom door. What I found was a brand new "big, brown" bedroom set, all setup, complete with a headboard, dresser, and desk. I was devastated; what should have been a wonderful present brought a flood of tears instead. I don't mean to sound ungrateful, but it was such a disappointment. The worst I have ever known. I knew my parents meant no harm and it was my own fault. I had allowed myself to dream and to assume that it was something it wasn't. This entire episode was a good lesson for me to learn how to avoid disappointment. From then on I vowed, "to never expect anything and then be surprised when something good comes my way." I never told my parents. It was my secret to bear.

All in all, life was idyllic in Andover, and I was always busy. But for me, there was still something missing—horses. It wasn't until I was in the 7th grade that my life in Andover started to make sense. I met a girl in my sewing class named Pam. The two of us did a decent job in making our aprons, but when we took the cooking class the next semester, we landed a solid "D" for our chocolate chip cookies. How can anyone get a "D" in cookie making? Well, for one thing, ours looked like a pepperoni pizza. And if I remember, they might have tasted like it, too.

As I got to know Pam more, I discovered that she loved horses as much as me, but she knew more about them than I did. She introduced me to an older man named Mr. Chester Abbott. He was married to a lady named Grace, and they didn't live far from town. Nobody did. Their house was down the hill from our church, under the "horn" bridge, which was a railroad track over the street. There was a sign painted on the bridge abutment that said to blow your horn before you went under the bridge so that drivers coming the other way would know you were entering. Hence the name, Horn Bridge.

Mr. Abbott had a big, old barn and owned several homes on his property. The barn was more than 100 years old back the 1960s, but it was magical to me, and it smelled like horses, which was no doubt due to Mr. Abbott boarding so many of the horses and ponies around town for other people.

Pam had been helping Mr. Abbott after school each day, and one day she asked me if I wanted to join her. I was so excited! My dream was finally coming true. I couldn't wait for school to get out so I could run home, jump on my bike and ride down to the old barn. My parents knew where I was and they knew I would be there all afternoon. In those days, you could come home when it was getting dark and no one ever worried.

Pam and I would groom the horses and clean the tack room. We would also clean out the stalls. In the old barn, there were trap doors in the floor between the stalls where we would throw the manure. From there it would drop down into the "basement" of the barn that opened up to a side driveway, and people would come to buy manure for their gardens. Every once in a while when Pam and I were in a joking mood, we would come up behind each other and push the other one down the trap door! We thought it was the funniest thing ever. However, my mother was not thrilled when I would come home later, covered in manure and stink up her house. On occasion, Mr. Abbott would even let us ride the horses in the small arena. It was like Heaven, and I was hooked!

Another job Mr. Abbott gave to us was collecting eggs from the henhouse. He raised these hens for their eggs and would sell them to the town folk. This one time, Pam and I decided to have an egg fight. It was a blast throwing them at each other and watching them drip down our hair and clothes. Mr. Abbott did not see the humor, however, and didn't ask us to collect the eggs anymore. I don't know how he had the patience to put up with us teenagers for as long as he did. He was such a wonderful man and a great mentor. Even Pam, although she was my age, was a great mentor to me.

One of the first horses we rode was Cocoa—a big, old chestnut horse. Pam and I would ride double bareback and walk the trails of the local Indian Reservation for hours in the summer and fall. The leaves would turn the most beautiful colors in the fall—stunning oranges, reds, yellows and browns. I can still hear them crunching under Cocoa's hooves when he walked us through them, still feel the soft breeze on my face, and still smell the beautiful fragrances of fall in New England. There was nothing like it in the world—or at least in mine.

Soon thereafter, Mr. Abbott acquired two ponies—Friskie, a tri-colored (brown, white and black) Shetland pony, and another black pony we called Snap. Friskie was a typical pony, feisty and stubborn, but so was I! He had met his match! Shortly after the ponies arrived, Mr. Abbott decided that he wanted to surprise his wife Grace, and he shared with me his plan. Later that same day, I climbed on Friskie and headed toward the Abbott's house. Mr. Abbott was waiting for me at the back door. When I got closer, he opened the door, and Friskie and I rode straight into the kitchen where Mrs. Abbott was cooking. As she looked up, it took her a few seconds to realize who and what had joined her, and she let out of scream. She was surprised, all right! The expression on her face was priceless, and the memory made us laugh for a long time after.

In the beginning, Pam would lend her knowledge and would give me a few "lessons" in the small area we called the "arena"—a cleared out sandlot surrounded by tall pine trees. The arena wasn't that big, but it suited the purpose for what was needed, as I learned the specifics of riding.

The farm next to Mr. Abbott's property was a dairy farm. The owner grew his own feed corn for the cows. In the summer when the corn was at its peak and ready to harvest, Pam and I would ride the ponies down all the rows of corn stalks—row after row—and we would laugh and chase each other around. It was so much fun! Then we would come out at the other end covered in corn silk and leaves. It was also a challenge to keep the ponies from eating the corn! It was "feed" corn for animals, and it tasted terrible, but the ponies didn't seem to notice and tried to eat it anyway.

On occasion, Pam and I would also ride the ponies over to Pomp's Pond, a pond (or it could have even been a small lake) just a few miles away from the Abbott's. We would ride through the old Girl Scout camp to the beach and then go directly into the water. Pam and I would even swim with the ponies, and no one seemed to care. Then we would make our way back to the barn in our soaked clothes and drenched ponies, and we giggled all the way home. It was quite a sight. Our little excursion was especially fun in the heat of summer on those sweltering, humid days when being outside was often too much to bear.

At long last, summer would fade and fall came in with all its glory. Leaves began to fall, and a cool breeze would fill the air. Our rides through the trails were picture perfect with all the beautiful colors and the smell of burning leaves in the air. People would rake the colored leaves into large piles and put them on the street curb. Then they would burn them to get rid of them all. Burning the leaves would be impossible to do today, because of all the regulations and fire codes, but oh what a special time it was back then.

Then winter would arrive with the first snow storm of the season—so beautiful, but so very cold. In the barn's tack room was an old potbellied stove. Mr. Abbott always had it burning hot on Saturday when we would come over to clean the stalls. As I look back on the memory, I cannot imagine starting a fire in the old stove inside a 100-year old, rickety wood building, but Mr. Abbott did it every day during the cold winter months, and it warmed us to our very souls. Knowing what was waiting for us, Pam and I would rush to clean stalls. Then we would run back to the tack room to get warm. Mr. Abbott would sometimes bring us hot chocolate and cookies. Such a sweet man he was and all great memories he left behind.

One of my favorite memories was when Mr. Abbott hitched Cocoa up to an old sleigh, and Pam and I climbed onboard with blankets piled high around us. He drove that sleigh up to the center of town and right down Main Street. I'll never forget that ride. The snow was coming down pretty good, and not many cars were out. The deserted streets belonged to us. I can still hear the sleigh's runners sliding across the snow-packed road. It was magical—a childhood memory that will forever be etched in my heart.

Then like clockwork, spring arrived New England style, with warm, balmy air and the aroma of all the different flowers, shrubs, and trees. I loved springtime at the barn. We would all spend hours cleaning out the tack room, then more hours as we cleaned and conditioned all the tack.

Spring was also a time for horse shows, and every young girl who loved horses wanted to be in them. Pam and I were no different. Several times, Mr. Abbott would board up the sides of his pickup truck, and somehow we got the two ponies in the back. Then off we went! Now mind you, Pam and I were still in the 7th and 8th grade, and these two animals were ponies. We might have looked a little too big for them, but we didn't care. I think we acquired several ribbons, but only because there were just six of us competing... and we came in 6th place. But it felt like 1st place to us. The ribbons were shiny, beautiful and green, and I felt as if I were in Heaven once again.

The next horse that Mr. Abbott acquired was a large pony, probably 14.2 hands, which is big for a pony. He was a dark bay, kind of a mahogany color. Pam had just gotten over a bout with mononucleosis, so we named the horse "Monohogany." We thought that was pretty darn clever! We took "Mono" to a show shortly after his arrival. I borrowed all the English clothing and knee boots that I needed from a neighbor girl. They didn't exactly go to my knees, and the clothes didn't fit very well, but it made no difference to me. Pam and I had a great time preparing for the event. Again, I think we "won" the same color ribbons once again, but it didn't matter. We were just happy to be part of the event. It was such a great experience and one that I will treasure for the rest of my life.

The last horse Mr. Abbott let us ride was a Paint tri-color horse. The owner had asked to board her, and he paid for six months up front, but he never came back (much to our delight). We named her Patches...original huh?

It didn't take long for us to recognize the signs that Patches had been abused. So Pam and I spent many hours retraining her and showing her the love that no one ever had before. She was the sweetest horse. I rode her everywhere. I would even ride her to my house and take her tack off, then let her graze in our fenced-in backyard. She loved to eat the grass. I can't remember my dad's reaction. (Maybe that's a good thing!) I would often pretend that she was mine and lived in my backyard. A girl can dream, can't she?

Soon Pam and I graduated from junior high and began our journey into high school. Because of our different classes and schedules, Pam and I couldn't spend as much time together. She had also purchased a young horse that summer which she planned to train, and she wasn't able to come to Mr. Abbott's barn anymore. We remained friends, and she was always willing to help me with new ideas on how to work with Patches. I wasn't able to spend as much time with Patches as I used to either, but the memories we made together were priceless.

In my junior year of high school, I received a phone call from Pam with crushing news. Mr. Abbott and his wife had been killed in a car accident on their way to their grandson's wedding. I was devastated. I still remember the funeral with the double caskets. The service was held in the church that most of the people in Andover attended—the Old South Church, established in 1711. I used to think the minister of the church (Reverend Noss) had been there since 1711—a humorous distraction in the midst of great sadness.

Not long afterward, everything on the Abbott property was auctioned off. I was thrilled to learn that Patches would be going to Mr. Abbott's son's family in Vermont. It was comforting to know that this beautiful horse would have another good home. But oh how I would miss her.

As I look back on this journey through my early years, I can see how God allowed these horses and the circumstances surrounding them to come into my life, including the precious friendship with Pam, Patches and dear Mr. Abbott. God genuinely cared about the desires of my heart, and Pam, Patches and Mr. Abbott all played their parts. And though I wasn't able to ride very much through my college and graduate school years, I never forgot the roots God had planted in my heart, and my desire for these magnificent animals never went away.

During a recent reunion with my sisters in 2018 (all of us in our 60s and 70s), I told them about this book I was writing. Georgia and Nancy immediately started to reminisce about their memories of my passion for horses. Apparently, I used to conduct a "horse school" in our house in Andover and my two "eager" students were Georgia and Nancy.

On the third floor, there were several old school desks—so I had a classroom. I would bring a few of my prize plastic horses up to the classroom. I also had pictures of horses and we would discuss their habits and go over their anatomy. This was interesting because I knew nothing other than what I was reading right along with my "students." But I was their teacher and I wanted them to know everything I knew (or thought I knew). It was the classic "fake it till you make it"...which I did.

Another memory they brought to mind were the hurricanes we used to have. Often times they were so severe that we all hightailed it to our big, cold basement for protection. But before we went downstairs, us girls would always grab something and take it with us that was important so if the house was ever blown away, we would still have our treasures with us. Of course, no one ever thought that if the house was blown away, so would we!

I'm sure you know what my treasures were and I boxed up every horse I owned and took them with me down to the basement. When the wind blew hard, I'm sure my first thought was protecting what I held dear, and no doubt laying my body over the boxes to keep them safe. Really?!

Remember, I had over 100 of these horses in that collection. Some big, some smaller. Some plastic, some porcelain, some wooden. All dearly loved. Whenever we went on vacation, I would always scour the gift shops for anything that looked like a horse.

I told you my mom sold my collection at a garage sale after I left for college. It hurt terribly and I wasn't sure I could ever truly forgive her. But today, as I look back, was I really going drag that collection into adulthood? My future husband would love it, wouldn't he? I don't think so.

So, I say this to you now, Mom. It's okay. I love you and I forgive you—and Dick thanks you!

CHAPTER 2

Life After the Abbott's

Not long after the Abbotts passed away, I started a job across the street from the old barn. It was at a dairy farm called Rose Glenn. We always referred to it as "Sid Whites" because he was the owner. The corn fields where Pam and I rode through with the ponies belonged to him, and he had a small dairy store where he would sell milk, eggs, and cream. He also made his own ice cream. I worked for him for a year and a half during high school, serving ice cream—one scoop at a time.

One day this little league team came in—all 23 of them. Every one of these kids ordered a banana split. They were celebrating their very first win in several years and getting ice cream was their prize. I was all by myself at the counter and never worked so hard in my life. In fact, I ran out of bananas and had to send someone to another store to buy more. Suffice to say, I have not been a fan of ice cream or bananas since.

The first summer after high school graduation, I had landed a job at the new Sheraton Rolling Green Hotel. It was owned by good friends of my parents, the Axelrods. I had formed a singing duet (in my senior year of high school) with a good friend named Jenny. We both played guitars—it was the 60s, after all—and we sang folk songs. We had both sung in the school talent shows, and we were looking for somewhere to continue our singing and maybe even make a little money too.

I really can't remember how it all came about, but Jenny and I got a job singing in the main dining room at the Sheraton Rolling Green, four evenings a week, from 5:00 to 9:00. We had such a great time, and the people seemed to enjoy us as well. I remember taping a piece of paper to the side of my guitar with the order of songs we would sing. Customers complimented our performance and even made song requests that they knew we had sung before. Jenny and I also managed to get a few tips too. Our six-week "gig" turned out to be a very delightful experience.

When it was over, I still had about a month before I went off to college. My sister Mollie was waitressing at the

Wentworth by the Sea in Portsmouth, NH. She didn't think I should be sitting around for a month—I thought it was a great idea. She won. Somehow Mollie was able to secure the high position of me waitressing for the other waiters and waitresses, serving them their meals before they went to work in the main dining hall. The room where I served the workers was called the "Side Hall". I didn't receive any tips from the other employees, but I was paid hourly for my work, which was always better than nothing.

The Wentworth was a fancy, old posh resort, where people (mainly from New York) would come for a week's vacation. There were dormitories on the property where all the employees would live, and it was quite an experience for a young gal like me, who grew up in a bubble in a little town. Many of the waiters were gay, although I don't think I even knew the word back then. Once I learned of its meaning, I never had an opinion one way or the other about their lifestyle. I was brought up not to judge—so I didn't.

Most of the folks I worked with were great people, and I had some good times there. I remember this one time being in one the men's rooms to pick something up, and I noticed a can of hairspray on the dresser. That surprised me! Back then, men didn't use hairspray; they used Brylcreem ("a little dab will do ya"), but, again, no judgment from me.

I was at the Wentworth for about a month. It was a great time of learning and also for stretching my mind. I had fun because my boyfriend Edd would come to visit and we would spend time together on the beach playing our guitars.

CHAPTER 3

Campfire Girls' Camp

From the very beginning after our arrival in Andover, my mom would send all four of us girls to Campfire Girls' camp called Camp Kiwanee near Cape Cod for two weeks of great fun. The camp was located on a beautiful lake, where we would take swimming and canoeing lessons. It was here that I learned to "gunnel". It's a word, I promise. Let me explain. Whenever we'd go out in the canoe, we'd sometimes lose a paddle. When this happened, we were taught to stand up on the sides (the gunnels or gunwales) at the back of the canoe, and then bend our knees and swing our arms in circles, pumping the canoe forward. It was fun and, not surprisingly, we would usually fall off, which was just as much fun.

There was a long list of activities to choose from, like archery and tennis, which I did quite often. There were also many arts and crafts classes that kept us busy in between all the sports. We lived in wooden cabins that were spread all over the property, usually around 6-8 girls in each room. Each cabin had screen coverings on a couple of the walls to help circulate the air inside and to keep the bugs out.

Every day we were allowed to go to the "store" and spend the money our parents had left for us in our accounts. My sisters' and my money was spent mostly on candy. Lots of candy, in fact! (Shhh). The "store" was quite the popular place for everyone. The camp also had "mail call" each day, and all the girls looked forward to this time as well. It was our only connection to the outside world and the life we left behind for two full weeks. My mom wrote to each one of us every day, so every day we each would receive a letter to read. It made us feel special and gave us something to look forward to.

The camp had several other opportunities we could do to keep us busy, like a trail ride on a horse, but the cost of these activities was extra. I begged my parents to let me go, and without too much convincing, they said okay. I was over the top ecstatic! It was such a wonderful gift for them to grant me this wish. This was long before I met Mr. Abbott so you can imagine my excitement.

On Thursdays after lunch, the group that was going on the trail ride was to meet on the steps of the old lodge/dining hall. The ancient camp station wagon (and I do mean ancient) would pull up in front, and we would all pile inside. Then we were driven to the stables where we were paired with the appropriate horse.

Most of the trail string horses were older than me and pretty slow, but I didn't care. I was on a horse! As I sat in the saddle and took it all in, I would stick my face into the horse's neck throughout the ride and then take in the biggest breath. I held it in as long as I could, for I knew that with this one breath, it had to last me the entire week.

The ride always seemed too short to me. When we arrived back in camp, it was almost time for the flag ceremony and dinner. I wanted the scent of that day to last forever, so I never bothered changing my clothes or washing my hands! I think I may have even slept in my clothes. With the aroma of horse and hay still lingering all around me after the lights went out, I would roll over in my bunk and dream about the next week's ride.

These summer getaways were precious to me, and I learned to do so many different things that would help me throughout my life. I also had the most amazing counselors at Camp Kiwanee—women that genuinely cared about me. There was one in particular who went great lengths to make sure I was on the right path for my education and my future. Her name was Jean Williams, but we all called her Miss "Willie."

Everyone looked up to Miss Willie, and everyone loved her—and rightly so. I truly believe God put this woman in my path, because He had great plans for my future, and He wanted her to help lead me there. Miss Willie had solid Christian values which I learned so much about the more time I spent with her. She was tons of fun, yet you knew where the line was drawn, and you respected it. I learned how to respect others because of her. Her bright smile and encouraging words were for everyone, and everyone adored her. But no one more than me!

The last summer I spent at Camp Kiwanee, I was in my sophomore year of high school. I applied for and was accepted to be a C.I.T. (Counselor in Training). That last year was a great experience and played a big part of helping me to stretch and grow. Soon after, I headed back home to begin my junior year. I knew I needed to start thinking about college, but after my high school guidance counselor met with me that year, I seriously doubted that I would ever go to college, or become anything worthy enough to do anything at all.

I have long since forgiven this woman, but it took me quite awhile. I will not stoop so low as to mention her name, even though I am quite sure she has long since passed. Her name is not important. It's what she said to me that crushed me to the core. Andover High School was an excellent school and had sent over 90% of its students to a 4-year college or university. Knowing these statistics gave me great hope.

My mom and I had met with my guidance counselor to talk about my future, which was part of her job (to guide me). She had been my guidance counselor since I started high school and she knew I needed help. My sister Mollie had been there just three years prior and had graduated with honors, which got her into a top-notch college. Then along comes Marcia—not the student of the year, or even for a day—wanting to know what was needed to get into a halfway decent college.

I honestly can't remember all that was said that day, but I do remember distinctly my "guidance" counselor saying to my mom, "Mrs. Anderson, your daughter Marcia will not only never get into college, but if by some fluke she ever does, she will never make it through." These were her exact words as I remember. Every word she spoke crushed me deeper. By the time I left her office, I felt three inches tall and good for nothing. I could not stop crying.

My mom, ever the defender, tried to make me feel better, and the guidance counselor to appear not quite so horrible by saying, "She knows you're a fighter, Marcia, and this was just a reverse psychology tactic." But I didn't buy it, not for one minute. And even though I did make it through college, I feel like I've spent much of my life proving this woman wrong. I even had, at one point, thought of sending her a copy of my Master's Degree Certificate, but decided against it. It wasn't important anymore.

The lesson was a tough one, but it was a lesson just the same. This entire incident taught me that what you say to someone really does matter, especially when talking to the young. Words can either lift and encourage or make someone feel hopeless and dejected. And though I have forgiven this person, I will never forget how she made me feel, and I vowed long ago never to let anyone feel that pain because of my thoughtless actions or words.

CHAPTER 4

Preparing for the Future

In my senior year, I began looking at colleges. Because my grades were not very good, I knew my choices were limited. Nonetheless, I still wanted a college with a good reputation for helping their students to be all they could be, no matter what the challenge.

Over the years, I had stayed in touch with Willie (as I called her later). She was someone you wanted in your life for as long as God allowed. Willie was from Ohio and had attended a small college in Northeast Ohio, called Hiram College. When I told her I was searching for a college, she recommended that I come to Ohio and visit Hiram. I flew out shortly after, and Willie picked me up and drove me to the college campus. It was about an hour northeast of Cleveland. Though Hiram College was small, its undersize appearance did not take away the beauty that stood before me when we pulled up. I was in awe. I quickly learned that there were less than 1000 students in attendance, and I prayed that I would soon be one of them.

Before my arrival, Willie had set up an interview for me. I was a nervous wreck. (Remember, a student I was NOT!) To my surprise—as much as everyone else's—the interview must have gone well because I was accepted! I kept thinking, "How did I do this?" The only thing I could come up with was that they must not have looked at my high school grades.

I went off to college still dating my boyfriend Edd. I was free, away from home, and 18 years old! In Ohio, you were allowed to drink 3.2 beer at 18. I just knew this law was designed especially for me, and you can bet that I had my share—the first semester. It was quite the experience. However, I did manage to squeeze in a few other things like, knitting a sweater for Edd during biology class and landing the supporting role in the class musical. Then, of course, more partying and beer with my newest "best" friends. College was great!

I went back home for the Christmas break anxious to see my family and friends. My grades arrived on Christmas Eve. On a 4-point scale, I received a .6—yes, a point 6—two Ds and an F. That great time I said I had and those beers I said I drank evidently showed in the reporting of my grades. My parents were not happy at all!

It was the 60s remember, and a lot of the kids were taking time off from college to "find" themselves. I suggested to my parents that maybe I might need to take a little time off from college to "find" myself, especially with my grades—or lack thereof—that were so low they were almost non-existent. This request did not deserve nor did it receive a response. Christmas was very quiet that year.

Monday morning came, and my father told me I was going to go to work with him and to be ready at 7:00. He also suggested that I bring a sack lunch because I would not be leaving the premises. We rode together in the car—in silence. It was the longest 30-minute ride of my life.

Once we arrived, my father took me to the assembly line at his coffee company. He introduced me to his foreman and then my dad said he'd see me at 5:00. The job was tedious and boring, but I did it, every day until it was time for me to return to school. And sure enough, I did find myself that winter break. I found myself putting bottles in boxes for all three weeks of my "vacation." And I found, too, that I didn't want that kind of life. My dad didn't have to say anything.

I got it!

When I returned to school, I was put on academic probation—duh! I could finally see clear enough to see the writing on the wall—no grades, no education, no future—and I woke up! The next semester I landed a 3.2. I learned you can "come back" and you can succeed. A hard lesson, but a necessary one—and I thank God and my parents for their guidance and grace.

CHAPTER 5

Essex Street

The following summer, my mother, who had always been good at planning my life, thought that I should have a summer job to keep me busy and out from under her feet. She had read an ad in our local newspaper, *The Lawrence Eagle Tribune,* about a need for recreation leaders at four housing projects in the town next to Andover. We four girls learned very early in life that we didn't say "No" to our mother, so off I went for an interview. Surprisingly, I landed the job! I was assigned to the Essex Street Housing Project, which was one of four low-income housing projects in Lawrence. The children who lived in this project were the ones who were desperate for entertainment, and my job was to work with these kids.

I worked from 9:00am to 4:00pm at one of the four apartment complexes. There were two of us at this complex, and we put together a game plan that produced a good solid program of activities. One of the things I organized was a rummage sale. I collected discards from my parents and their friends and our neighbors, and then sold them at the apartment complex. All the money went into equipment for the kids. One summer we raised enough money to take four buses (one from each complex) to a Red Sox game.

My co-worker and I were in charge of 200 kids (ranging from grade school up to high school). I still don't know how we did it! Getting everyone on a bus and accounted for, traveling about 45 minutes to Fenway Park, unloading and keeping a group of 200 children together. Then watching the game, loading them back on the correct bus, and accounting for each kid was all a bit stressful, but uneventful. I know without a doubt that the Lord's hands were definitely in this great journey. From start to finish, it was indeed a miracle!

As it turned out, one of the kids ended up on the wrong bus, but the bus driver took notice and brought him back to his apartment complex without incident. I went home with a massive headache, but it was all worth it in the end.

The following summer I went back to the complex and ended up having the same partner from the year before. We worked well together, so I was happy he was with me again. The third summer I was the only one to return. I can't remember exactly how it all came together but, by the last summer, I was in charge of all four apartment complexes with two helpers at each complex to work with. By this time, we had developed a full program of recreational activities for the children. The City had given us a budget to work with for all our supplies and equipment.

My fourth and last summer I wanted to make as much money as I could, so I asked Mr. Axelrod (the owner) if I could work at his Sheraton Rolling Green again. He was kind enough to give me a job in the main dining room Monday through Friday, and he opened the Coffee Shop on Saturdays for me so that I could waitress. I worked the Recreation (kids) job from 9-4, and the coffee shop from 5-10. What was I thinking? I was exhausted by the end of the summer, but I had made good money which I needed for school.

The last night at the restaurant, the bartender wanted to make me something special to celebrate my last day, so he made me a Long Island Iced Tea. I had never had one of these before—or since. Need I say more?

CHAPTER 6

College and Beyond...

During my college years, I must have changed my major ten times. I started out to be an elementary education major. At one point, I even spent the day with my sister Mollie's classroom thinking it could help give me an idea of what it would be like teaching. After a full day of being with 20-plus first graders, I was exhausted. When I got home, I went straight to bed and slept all night. I didn't even wake up for dinner. It was a no-brainer that I wasn't cut out to teach little children.

That next semester, I went back to school and changed my major again—this time to psychology. I thought maybe I could learn how to "psyche" people out! But that didn't work either. Giving this a little more thought, I realized I still wanted to teach, just not elementary school. I had played all the college sports—basketball, volleyball, and tennis—and was even "captain" of the Hiram Tennis Team.

Of course, my youngest sister Nancy was captain of the Stanford Tennis Team…I'll say no more. Still this experience with sports and the love of teaching, I thought to myself, "Maybe I'll be a Physical Education teacher!" That should be pretty easy, right? Wrong! I found out that I had to take biochemistry and kinesiology! Unfortunately for me, I had already put in for it, and it was too late to change to another major and still be able to finish in four years. And I was pretty sure my parents would not entertain the idea of me doing a fifth year!

The final I had to take for kinesiology was brutal. I was to show where the "origins" and "insertions" were for all the muscles from the waist up, while a swimmer was swimming the "free-style stoke". Are you kidding me? I thought. I couldn't tell you today if my life depended on it what I wrote for my answers. I had elected to take this course for a "pass or fail" grade. I knew that a "D" was passing, but the word "pass" looked much better than seeing a "D" on my report card. And, not surprisingly, it looked much better than seeing the word "fail" or an "F". Well, I passed! And I thanked God for His hand in it all. This was truly another one of His miracles and I was forever grateful. I didn't graduate with honors, but I did graduate with a double degree in Health and Physical Education from Hiram College in Hiram, Ohio!

The four summers I spent at Essex Street Complex was an incredibly satisfying experience—so much so, that I decided to go on to grad school and major in Parks and Recreation. However, there were three obstacles that stood in my way; money, the fact that I was not a great student, and that I had to take the Graduate Record Exam (GRE). Plus I realized that I could have a slight problem with the math questions on the GRE. I hadn't had a math class for four years. It was not a requirement at my college to take any math to graduate, and if it wasn't required, why would I take it? But what the heck, I thought I should at least give it a try. So I did. I had a wonderful Biology teacher who was a great encourager. She had attended Indiana University and said they were just beginning a Graduate Program in Public Parks and Recreation Administration. I also did some research and discovered that the University of Connecticut also had a program.

The first thing I did was apply at both schools. Then I scheduled to take the Grad Report Exam at Case Western Reserve University in Cleveland. I drove in the night before and stayed in a friend's dorm room at Case. His name was

Rookie Valentine. Rookie and I had grown up together in Andover and we were great friends... so much so that we spent the night reminiscing, and staying out partying into the early morning hours. Not a very smart thing to do, but then again, I was not a very smart person back then. Still, I dragged myself into the testing classroom to take the exam. It was all a blur.

They gave you two choices for test results; to receive your test scores by mail, or to have them sent straight to the school where you applied. I didn't want to know my results, so I had them sent to the University of Connecticut and to Indiana University. You can imagine my shock when I was admitted to both schools! My parents were beyond shocked! After my dad told me how proud he was of me, he asked how I was going to pay for it. I told him I had a plan.

I had applied to Indiana University to be a Resident Assistant (RA) in the dorms. I was accepted and it was a full assistantship. It paid for everything except my books, which I knew my summer jobs would pay for. Watch out Bloomington, Indiana. Here I come!

Most of the graduate classes I was taking, I thoroughly enjoyed. They were fun and interesting and I actually wanted to be there. I chose to be there, and I worked hard to get there. I received above average grades in all my classes—well, except in statistics.

I am not, nor have I ever been a morning person. This class started at 7:30am in the dead of winter, which meant it was still pretty dark when I went to class. It nearly took an act of God to get me to class, and then I had to force myself to sit in the front so I wouldn't fall asleep. I think you get the idea.

After all these years, I was finally taking this schooling stuff seriously and was willing to do whatever was necessary to make sure my grades stayed up. I seem to recall that I had even dated one of my professor's sons for a while. I can't remember the grade I got in his father's class, but I don't think I scored any extra credit by dating his son. Go figure.

CHAPTER 7

Goodbye Single Life ....
Hello Dick

While attending school in Indiana, I met my husband Dick. Actually, it's where I "re-met" him. Dick and I had grown up together in Andover. He was two years ahead of me in school, and he attended Phillips Academy Prep School for Boys in Andover. We went to the same church, and belonged to the same youth group, "Pilgrim Fellowship".

Somewhere in those first few years we were in Andover, my family had met the Cromie family. Helen and Gil Cromie had a son named Dick and a daughter named Janet. Janet was my sister Georgia's age. Helen (I called her Mrs. Cromie back then) became a household name in our family. She was a teacher by trade, and all of us girls had her as a substitute in our various classrooms. Mrs. Cromie was never mean, but she was very stern, which made her somewhat scary.

We were all afraid of her. She meant business but she had a loving encouraging side to her too. Mrs. Cromie was also one of my Sunday school teachers, and she shared the role of leadership as Campfire Girls' leader with my mom.

Dick and I attended the same youth group at church, but because he went to Phillips Academy we didn't interact much. When I was a sophomore in high school, Dick and I double dated to the prom. Dick went with my friend Paula (she had invited him), and I went with a fellow named Pedrick. Dick drove us all in his shiny, new dark green Ford Galaxy convertible with a white top.

Over the years, Dick dated my friend Ginny who was my tennis-doubles partner in high school. So suffice to say, Dick and I knew each other fairly well, but we were just friends. Life went on and we both went off to college and careers. I went to Indiana for my graduate work and Dick had landed a job with Westinghouse in Bloomington, Indiana of all places. (God was at work).

Our parents, being friends, suggested that we look each other up. We didn't. I guess our recollections of one another weren't very positive. I remember Dick as a quiet, bookworm type—very smart, yet rarely talked. He remembered me as the "party girl", which I think translated into "a loud, obnoxious ADD girl."

One day, Dick's parents decided to visit their son in Indiana, and they asked if there was anything they could bring me from my parents since they were coming anyway. I asked them to ask my mom for my big, yellow, fluffy comforter that I had to leave behind because it wouldn't fit in my car when I drove to school.

They brought it, and Dick called a short time later to tell me he had my blanket. He was cute when he invited me to have a beer with him so that he could make his delivery. We met a couple nights later and spent the entire time talking and catching up. Over the next year, we remained the best of friends and even fixed each other up with other people to date.

It was easy for me to set Dick up because I knew he'd make a good catch for someone. Not only was he handsome, but he owned his own 3-bedroom ranch-style house—and he had a boat! We continued our match-making relationship setting up one another with someone we thought the other would like. Dick and I ended up being known as the "couple" who planned many parties and boat excursions and always having a special someone for the other person. When I went home for the summer, Dick wrote to me at least once a week—this was before computers and cell phones. He also has a habit that annoyed my mom terribly. He would call to talk to me, but he never paid much attention to the time, forgetting that we were an hour later, and my folks were sleeping.

The two of us picked up where we left off when I returned by match-making and introducing our best friends (Ken and Judy) to each other. Ken worked with Dick at Westinghouse, and Judy was an RA (Resident Assistant) with me in the only all women's dorms on campus called Forest Quad. Eleven-story towers on each side and no air conditioning! Fortunately for me, I was at the end of the hall on the second floor with a huge shade tree in front of my window. Not that I ever spent that much time in my room studying, but at least the shade was there—in case. The Midwest humidity could be brutal. Thank God the lounges, dining halls, classrooms, and library were all air-conditioned (though I didn't spend much time in the library either).

When I came back in the fall for my last semester, Dick and I both realized there was something going on between us. I was in love with him and, as it turned out, he was in love with me, though neither of us knew. He was a happy bachelor at 25, but God had other plans. We had never actually said "I love you" out loud. Our letters always ended in "love", but I signed that way with lots of friends, so for me, it wasn't really a commitment.

During the spring of 1972, Dick and I had several parties at his house and on the boat at Lake Monroe. We invited lots of couples, some married, but no one had any kids. We rented this pontoon boat for the day. We had a picnic and water skied off Dick's boat. When Dick first bought his boat, it had already been named "Scotty", but soon after we decided to rename it "Bay State", which is what Massachusetts is called (classy huh?).

On May 22 of that year, Judy and I threw a surprise birthday party for Dick. I helped make lasagna in Judy's un-air-conditioned apartment. We were literally in our underwear putting these layers of lasagna together. It was sweltering. A funny side note: Not long after we were married, Dick was asked, "What was the one thing that drew you to Marcia?" He answered, "Her lasagna!" I laughed because it was actually Judy who made the lasagna—it was her recipe. A few years later, I asked Dick, "Have I made you any lasagna since we've been married?" He thought for a minute, then he said, "Well, no..." To this day, I don't think I've ever made him lasagna. But I got the guy!

Not long before my last semester in graduate school started, Ken and Judy announced their engagement. We were so excited for them. (They have been together for more than 45 years, and have three grown children and a boatload of grandchildren).

Three weeks later, Dick and I were hosting a party at his house in September. While we were both running around making sure everybody had what they needed, we ended up bumping into each other in the dining room. You can imagine my surprise when Dick put his hands on my shoulders, looked me straight in the eye, and said, "Will you marry me?"

The first words out of my mouth were, "Are you drunk?" (Romantic, huh?) But I had to make sure. Once I realized he was serious, I was in shock! Then he took me by the hand and led me into the bedroom, and closed the door. I quickly took a seat on the bed before I fell down.

"Are you going to answer me?" Dick asked sweetly. I looked up at him and, not surprisingly, I said "Yes!" Then I heard a scream from the other side of the door. It was Judy. She had been avoiding me all evening because Dick had told her that he was going to ask me, and she didn't want to accidentally ruin the surprise. When I opened the door, Judy grabbed me and gave me the biggest hug. It didn't take long for the news to travel through the house. Our friend Rudy ran up to Dick and asked him, "What have you done? Do you know what you're doing?" I guess he wanted to make sure Dick wasn't drunk either. We still laugh about that today.

That night I went back to the dorm feeling as if I were floating on air. I still couldn't believe it. We hadn't even really had a "formal" date. Up to this point, it had always been kind of "group" dating. Dick had never asked me out, picked me up, or brought me home. And we still had never said the actual words "I love you" to one another. But it was plain to see we did! Who'da thunk!

CHAPTER 8

Planning a Wedding

I've always heard, "If you want to make God laugh, tell Him your plans." My plans were to graduate in December from Indiana University, and then find a job locally and see if things developed between Dick and me. But Dick was way ahead of me (I liked his plan better.)

We called my parents to share with them the "Good News", and they told us that they had a feeling it was going to happen soon. Then we called Dick's parents. I told Dick I wanted to listen in on the conversation while he shared our news of our engagement. I asked him not to tell them I was listening.

The three of them chatted a while. I was getting antsy and kept mouthing to Dick, "Tell them!" Finally, Dick said, "When you come to visit next month, you can meet my fiancée." Dead silence. Oh no! This cannot be good. It was probably only a few seconds before the silence was broken, but it felt like an eternity. Gil finally said, "And you had to go all the way to Indiana to get her!" Helen was confused and asked, "Who is it, Gil?" She must have said it five times before he finally said in his New England accent, "It's Maaasha." Silence again. What was I thinking being on the phone listening? Maybe Helen didn't like the little Anderson girl.

What seemed like a lifetime later, she said, "Oh, how wonderful!" Whew, I started to breathe again. Then she asked, "Can we talk to her?" And, of course, 'honest' Dick replied, "Oh, she's been on the phone the whole time." I was hoping there was a hole in the floor that would open up and swallow me.

The four of us have laughed several times about that conversation. Helen asked me once, "What if I would have said, 'Oh you don't want to do that!' or something else really awful." I just blew it off and told her, "But you didn't. You accepted me; you invited me in to be part of your family and have loved me all this time." (I felt very blessed to have had such a wonderful relationship with my dear in-laws.) Now we had a wedding to plan.

I had always thought I wanted to have a big, fancy

wedding. I remember going through that summer when my sister Mollie was getting married and watching her and my mother "interact". It was an interesting time. On the day of her wedding, we were in my parents' bedroom getting ready. This room had the only window air conditioning in the entire house. When the phone rang, my mom picked it up. She didn't say a word. She didn't have to. We knew immediately that something was wrong. Then she turned a chalky white and looked as though she was going to be sick. "What, Mom?" Mollie asked. My mom hung up the phone and told us the news. "The catering truck has been in an accident. It flipped over in the intersection outside of town." Oh, dear, this was not good.

But instead of panicking, a call went out to family and friends, and they all pitched in. In the end, everyone brought a dish of some sort and the reception and dinner turned out absolutely perfect as if it had been planned. It probably even tasted better than what the caterers could have done because everything there was made with love.

The memory of this incident helped me to realize that a big wedding wasn't my desire any longer. Way too stressful. Dick and I also decided we wanted to get married in Indiana, and we asked our parents if they minded. Surprisingly, they all agreed. I think it was a relief, especially for my mom. Our guest list back home would have been overboard, to say the least. Our parents' only request was that we were married in a church, and we definitely knew we could do that!

Our friends Ken and Judy set their wedding date for the end of June of 1973. I wanted to get married on my parents' 30th anniversary, which was April 11, 1973, but that was a Wednesday. We settled for that coming Saturday, April 14th.

At last, I was engaged and the wedding was set! However, we still needed the symbol that would show everyone that I was spoken for—not that anyone was breaking any doors down or anything…

Dick took me ring shopping, or maybe I dragged him to the local jewelry stores. I loved looking at all the different diamond rings. I ended up picking out two designs that were my favorites, and I asked Dick to surprise me with his decision. He asked curiously, "So, how big does this diamond have to be?" I replied simply, "I just want to be able to see it."

I wondered when and how he would give my ring to me, but I didn't have to wonder very long. One night I was deep into my studies attempting to write a paper. Well, maybe not deep into it. Remember, a student I was not! Dick called me on the phone, and said, "Let's go get a bite to eat." And, of course, anything that would distract me from this paperwork, I was all for doing. "Give me ten minutes!" I responded, probably a little too anxiously.

I was dressed and ready, and my ever-so-prompt fiancé was right on time. Dick drove us to a quaint, little Italian restaurant downtown. There were lovely tables with white linens over the top and fresh flowers in the center of each one.

After the hostess seated us, I noticed Dick acting a little nervous, although it didn't dawn on me at the time why he would be. He ordered us some wine and appetizers. Then he reached into his pocket and took out a small, square box. Of course, I knew exactly what it was and I gasped excitedly. I don't remember breathing until he opened it and I saw my real engagement ring. It was stunning—so delicate and sparkly.

The band was a white gold, and on top sat a beautiful diamond solitaire, which I could see quite well. It was surrounded by a ring of sapphires, similar to one of the designs I had picked out, but not quite the same. Instead of having a ready-made one, my sweet fiancé had my ring custom made to suit me, and I loved it!

Talk about being in Heaven! At this moment in time, I was right there. I had a beautiful ring given to me by the man I loved and adored. I was over the moon. It was all really happening! Now all we needed was to find a place to have our special day.

Dick and I had been attending (very sporadically) a small Methodist church, and we asked the pastor if he would marry us. He agreed and said he would like to meet with us three times prior to the wedding. We met with him once, and he basically told us, "You both are doing great. See you on the 14th!"

Shortly after, Judy and I went looking for wedding dresses. I was beyond excited. I felt like a little girl playing dress up. Needless to say, I was much thinner back then (size 8-10), but I have never been a frilly person. However, the style at the time was frilly. I looked everywhere and I couldn't find anything that I wanted. Not sure if I mentioned that Judy was an excellent seamstress. Seeing my disappointment, my friend offered to make my dress. It was an A-line, empire waist, satin dress. The fabric cost all of $30. I put some white lace with purple ribbon through it to go with my color theme which was all lavenders and purples. Even my invitations were purple on lavender parchment paper.

My mom was not very happy. By now she was a full-fledged New Englander and truly believed that "white is right". I learned later that Helen didn't care for purple at all, which meant neither would be wearing purple for my wedding. They both chose blue, but I didn't care. I was getting married! Someone loved me!

CHAPTER 9
My Wedding Day

I was up fairly early the morning of April 14, 1973. My three sisters, my parents and I were all staying at the Howard Johnson—the only hotel in Bloomington, Indiana at the time. We were all famished so our group decided to go downstairs to the coffee shop and get some breakfast.

The Howard Johnson in my hometown was not known for their speedy service, and this one here in Bloomington didn't seem to be any better. After waiting much too long for our food, my mother announced in a very loud voice, "I think they pay these people to be slow!" I wanted to crawl under the table, I was so embarrassed. Needless to say, this incident has been very good for many a laugh over the years. After breakfast was over and the bill was paid, my entire wedding party on my side all went to have our hair done at the local salon. It was quite the sight when ten of us walked in. We had appointments, but still, it was a long process to make us all beautiful enough for my wedding day. Back then, we had to do our own makeup as it wasn't a perk that any salon had offered yet.

I had six bridesmaids; my three sisters, my soon to be sister-in-law, Janet, my best friend from college, Sue, and my best friend from grad school, Judy. Poor Dick had to scramble to find enough groomsmen to escort this tribe!

We were married at Saint Mark's Methodist Church in Bloomington. There were about 60 people in attendance. It was the perfect number. I remember gripping my father's arm as we walked down the aisle, to the tune of the organist playing, "Here Comes the Bride." I have always been fairly traditional. With each step I took, I remember thinking how good and right this felt, as I got closer to the man I loved and would spend my life with from this day forward. I never had any doubts and still don't after 45 years. I was about to marry my best friend. Does it get any better than this?

When we had our initial meeting with the minister about the ceremony, neither Dick nor I were into having a long, drawn-out service. We basically said, "Get us in and out of the church as fast as you can!" I am sure God was there with us through it all, although, to be honest, I never really thought about it until much later. When we had our 25th wedding anniversary party, we renewed our vows knowing that the God we served was present in all His glory. I don't remember ever feeling nervous—I was just so excited to be exiting the church as Mrs. Richard J. Cromie, and each step I took brought me closer to this reality.

The ceremony was short and sweet just like we wanted. Dick and I both loved the song "Danny Boy" so we asked Sally—a music major at Indiana University—if she would sing it for us. Naturally, she agreed and she sang the song beautifully. Listening to the words, you'd probably wonder about our sanity as to why we would choose this particular song. To be honest, I'm not really sure, but I do know that we both wanted it, so we included it.

As the words rang out and filled the church, I turned and walked over to each of my "mothers" and gave them a single white rose, and then kissed them both on the cheek. When I leaned over to my mom, I noticed the tears in her eyes. She told me later that "Danny Boy" had been her mother's favorite song. God works in mysterious ways. He knew all along that this song needed to be sung at our most special occasion.

After we said our vows, it was time for Sally to sing "The Lord's Prayer." The church grew quiet as they listened to each word. You might have even heard a pin drop had it not been for the music. It was beautiful and everyone watch as Sally sang her heart out. Then suddenly, without warning, in the middle of one of the most reverent verses, Doug, our best man, fainted! I looked over at Dick thinking he would do something, but he didn't move. In fact, all he could do was stare at his friend lying on the floor. It wasn't long before the minister and a couple of groomsmen bent down to help Doug up. But a few minutes later, he fainted again! It was a sight to be seen! This time they waited until Doug was fully awake before helping him to stand and get his bearings so that we could resume the ceremony.

I have no idea why our best man fainted—maybe there was too much excitement for him, though he certainly added some excitement of his own that day when he went down. Doug, who had been raised Jewish, told us later that when he woke up and saw that big wooden cross right above him, he wasn't sure what was going on! To this day, we still laugh about this, and Doug and his wife Susanna are still good friends of ours.

For our reception, there weren't a lot of options in

Bloomington, but there was no way I was going to have our blessed event at the Howard Johnson. So Dick and I hosted the reception at our home. It was perfect. We hired a lady to do the flowers, the cake, and the finger sandwiches—all for less than $500. I believe my dad was ecstatic!

Everything went beautifully and everyone looked like they were enjoying themselves. Dick and I greeted all our guests. We cut the cake and shared it with everyone. I wanted this night to last forever! But all good things must come to an end…eventually.

Back "in the day" it was customary not to leave the reception before the bride and groom. Everyone was still having a grand old time when my mother (aka Emily Post) approached us and said that our guests were getting hungry and wanted to go to dinner. We had only been married a few hours, but since my mom said it was time to leave, I guess we were supposed to leave.

The two of us went in the house to change our clothes, then came back to thank everyone for celebrating our special day. After that, we hopped in our new maroon Oldsmobile Cutlass Coupe that Dick had surprised me with the week before, and slowly backed out of the driveway. As we were driving away, everyone stood out front and threw the "traditional, well-wishing rice"—*lots* of it, in fact!

We didn't get far when we heard this strange noise coming from the backseat, and neither of us could figure out what it was. As we neared the top of the hill, one of our friends who decided to tag along, made himself known. After we all stopped laughing, Dick promptly stopped the car and told him to get out, to which our friend responded by throwing even more rice on us!

When we came home the next day, there was rice everywhere. It was even in the pill bottles we had in the medicine cabinet! Don't ask me how it got in there, but it did. I think we found rice in our suitcases for several years after. It was a grand celebration, and one we will always remember.

Because we both had to work that Monday after the wedding, Dick and I decided not to go on a honeymoon. We chose, instead, to spend our wedding night at the beautiful Brown County Inn in the next town over. Once we arrived at our room, Dick unlocked the door and then ceremoniously picked me up and carried me over the threshold. I felt like a queen. Of course back then I was a whole lot lighter, which made it easier for him to do. When Dick put me down, both of us noticed the several bottles of champagne sitting on the counter. We were thrilled that our friends had sent them over so that we could continue the celebration alone and making several toasts to our new life together.

We had a lovely dinner in the restaurant at the Inn before "retiring" for the night (wink, wink). I knew I had married exactly who God had chosen for me. And oh, that honeymoon? We never did take a traditional one—we didn't need to. Because today we are still on one—45 years and counting!

CHAPTER 10

Our Life

Indiana was our home for seven years. Dick was employed with the Westinghouse Corporation, and I had found a job working for the Girl Scouts local council. I met a woman named Dora who worked in the office. She had a sister who had a Plantation Walking horse, and oh, what a ride he was! Smooth as glass and huge as a…well, horse! This giant was 17 hands plus. To my delight, God had once again provided me with my heart's desire—another horse to love. I don't recall his name as he wasn't in my life long enough, nor was he ever my horse. However, I will never forget that feeling of being so moved by such a grand animal.

In 1978, Dick accepted a transfer to Southern California. I had just found out that I was pregnant with our first son, Michael. Prior to getting married, Dick and I had the "talk" about me being a "stay at home mom" when we started having kids. This was my time and I was going to do it with great passion and joy.

We moved to a small town about 30 minutes east of Los Angeles, called Diamond Bar. We chose Diamond Bar because there were two other Westinghouse couples living there, which gave us instant friends. Sandy, one of the wives, came to see us as we were moving all our stuff inside. She noticed my guitar case and asked if I played. I told her, "No, I just like carrying a guitar case around!" Then I laughed and she laughed with me.

Sandy told me about the guitar group at her church and said that I should investigate. All I heard was the word "Church", and it did not sit well with me. I had grown up in the Old South Church in Andover, and Dick and I were married in the Methodist Church. But I had never really attended church as an adult on a regular basis—ever!

I knew I believed in God, but I really didn't know very much about the Christian faith. Nonetheless, I loved playing the guitar and singing, so I pushed away whatever my mind was saying and listened to my heart instead. I ended up going to church and joining the singing group which called themselves "Of One Accord" (Catchy huh?)

Dick would come along occasionally when I asked him to. We both felt it was important to have our children attend church and learn about God. This was the beginning of our deeper walk with the Lord.

Six and a half years after Michael was born, we had our second son, Scott. Life was good. We were a happy family. We loved our beautiful home and living in Diamond Bar. We even had a pool for entertaining our family and friends. And, naturally, the boys loved it too.

When Michael and Scott started school, I found myself with a great deal "alone" time on my hands so I went seeking something to fill it. There was an older couple at church who had two horses that they didn't ride anymore, and I offered to exercise them. Low and behold, God provided once again for me to live my dream. This couple eventually moved away, but another member of our church had a horse and asked me if I could ride it for her. She didn't have to ask twice! God is so good.

The years we spent in Diamond Bar went by ever so quickly, and we made wonderful friends and memories that I will cherish forever. But after 15 years, we decided it was time to find a bigger home and moved one town over to San Dimas. Michael and Scott had been attending Sonrise Christian School, and San Dimas was a closer commute.

CHAPTER 11

Be Careful What You Pray For

"A righteous man cares for the needs of his animals."
(Proverbs 12: 10)

I'm one of those people who believe that God reigns supreme and that He has a grand plan for us all. As I look back on the years, I can see all the people I needed, who were put in my pathway purposefully—one of them being my best friend, my husband of 45 years...Dick. He and I both shared a love of horses. However, my kind was the hay eating kind and his was the gas eating kind.

I loved all breeds of horses, but Dick only had room in his heart to love one—Mustangs. He had owned and restored many of these classic cars over the years. Up to this point, I had never actually owned my own horse, yet always felt very blessed to have been around them most of my life. When I was 45, what I had prayed for all my life actually came true. I finally became a horse owner!

My sister Nancy was a physical therapist who did

home health care. She had a patient down the street from our house that bred and raised Quarter horses. When I learned that this patient of hers had horses and that he was obviously unable to give them any attention at this time, I asked my sister to tell him if he needed any help that I'd love to step in.

Nancy mentioned this to her patient, Tet Foster, but he wasn't very responsive at first. I was so disappointed and thought that maybe it wasn't meant to be. I put it behind me as best as I could, but it wasn't easy. Then on Nancy's very last visit with Tet (she was actually getting ready to walk out the door), he asked her if I was still interested in helping him. She was literally within seconds of walking out of this man's life forever—that was not a coincidence!

As soon as my sister told me the news, I wasted no time at all in calling Tet so that we could meet. I'll never forget how we started. When I got to his place, he told me to go into the small field and bring out the red dun horse (fortunately I knew my colors). The horse's name was Knothead, which should have given me a clue as to what I was in for.

I brushed and saddled Knothead as Tet stood by and watched closely. It was challenging at first because I grew up riding English in New England and this was a Western saddle. It was obvious to the owner that my memory was a bit out of practice, but I was determined to make this happen. After a while, it all came back to me (with a few hints from Tet, and a lot of patience). To this day, I don't know why this man had me take Knothead back down to the pasture with all the other horses, but he did. I went inside with Knothead and closed the gate; then I mounted and started to walk. The other four or five horses inside evidently thought it was an opportunity to run and play. Not surprisingly, my mount wanted to do the same—so off we went. Yet somewhere in my memory bank, I remembered how to stop a runaway horse—by turning the horse in a circle—which is what I did. After we stopped, I backed him up, thus attempting to show him who was in control. Even though I was a bit shaken, I felt good about the way I had handled the situation. Maybe Tet was testing my abilities (which were very rusty). However, I must have passed, because he allowed me to come back and help him.

I found out that Knothead was actually Tet's granddaughter's horse. She was in high school and started to love boys more than horses (something I could never imagine)! His granddaughter approached me one day and asked if I wanted to buy Knothead. Are you kidding me? I thought. "Yes" would have been my immediate answer as I was thrilled, to say the least. But I had one problem—Dick. How could I convince my husband to buy me a horse? It wouldn't be easy, but I could argue the fact that he had his own "horse"—a '67 Mustang convertible, so why not me too? I knew I had to use my words and timing perfectly, so I prayed. I gave it to the Lord and He gave me the words. I ended up using a word picture that I had learned at a church retreat one year.

"Now, Dick," I said, "I want you to picture the most pristine cherry Mustang you have ever seen…" He had this blank stare and said nothing, so I continued. "What would that car look like?" He only had to think for a few seconds before he described it in detail. Then I asked, "How badly would you want it?" Without hesitation, he admitted, "It's the car of my dreams."

I felt I had his attention, so I went on. "Well, I have this rare opportunity to acquire something that I, too, have always dreamed of…a horse!" My husband stared at me again, yet I couldn't quite read his expression…until he smiled. He had understood. I was ecstatic. I don't think I had ever hugged him so hard.

I floated on air for days! I had waited 45 long years for

this very moment! I was finally going to own my own horse. It was truly a dream come true. From that moment on, everything just fell into place, as if "Someone" else was in control. I was able to keep Knothead at the Foster's Ranch. I bought my own horse feed and cleaned my own stall. Tet didn't want me to pay board, so I helped around the yard and house. Tet, his wife Ramona and two of their sons (Leonard and Jack) became lifelong friends.

Jack was a Farrier—a person who shoes horses. He and his wife Betsy lived up in Bishop, CA, about four hours north of us. Jack came down about every six weeks to shoe the horses in the area, and he would always stop by and shoe Knothead. Jack taught me so much. He was very patient and I was like a sponge. Jack also had trained many horses under his father's experienced, watchful eye, and he was kind enough to share what he knew with me. Jack was the brother I never had.

As time went by, I started having friends ask me if I would teach their children how to ride. I was an accredited teacher by trade (in P.E.) and I loved teaching kids. Again my knowledge was a bit rusty, so I found a horse trainer in Orange County and took some classes that she offered to help my skill set. I started off teaching kids to ride Knotty.

He wasn't the perfect lesson horse but he was a good learner. People had offered to pay me too! I didn't feel worthy or qualified to take anyone's money, but Dick convinced me that it might help cover some of my costs. So I accepted. I think I started out charging around $10 an hour.

Somewhere along the way, I was asked if I wanted to purchase a pony that someone else had outgrown. I never dreamed I would own more than one horse! I took my friend Kash with me, who was a real trainer and horse-show judge to see this pony, Rusty Carousel. He had a bit of a limp and Kash wasn't sure if it would be a good buy or not. Plus they wanted $2500 for him. I don't know why I even went to see Rusty. I certainly didn't have $2500, and there was no way that I was going to ask Dick for it. So we came home and I didn't think any more about that cute pony.

About two months later, Rusty's owner called. She wanted me to know that she had dropped the price to $1000, and she assured me that he was sound (which meant he was no longer limping). Jack happened to be visiting, so we borrowed a trailer and went to see Rusty again. Before I went, I asked my sister Nancy if I could borrow $1000, and promised to pay her back. She readily agreed.

Jack rode Rusty. (Jack is short and Rusty was a tall

pony at about 13.2 hands). The pony looked great and Jack approved. Having cash in hand, I decided that I would try my hand at bargaining with the owners. I had never attempted this before, and I really wanted to tell Dick that I bargained the price down. Well, she ended up taking $950, and though it wasn't much, $50 is still $50. We brought Rusty back to the Foster's Ranch and a new chapter began.

One of the challenges of owning two horses was that I now needed tack for two...two saddles, two bridles, two of everything. Suddenly I could see more clearly why I needed to start taking money for the lessons.

CHAPTER 12
Horsey Business

My "business" started to grow and I felt so blessed. At the time, I was teaching P.E. to 7th and 8th graders at Sonrise Christian School. When the principal of the Junior High School realized I taught horseback riding, she asked if I would teach an elective class on horsemanship. This was such a great opportunity for me to show these kids my passion, as well as to share my knowledge of these animals that I loved so much! And best of all, my students loved learning.

I taught this class two days a week; one day was in the classroom, and one day I would bring the horse to school. The students were given the chance to groom the pony (I usually brought Rusty), but mostly they learned how to be around a horse, which many of them had never been exposed to. Jack would also come and demonstrate how to shoe a horse.

The word around the school spread quickly and everyone knew that I was teaching horsemanship and that I had horses. One day this woman, who ran the cafeteria, shared with me about her daughter who used to ride but had lost interest when she grew older. Since this horse was no longer being ridden, this woman asked if I would have any interest in taking her—at no cost! Free horse? How could I refuse? It's just another halter, saddle, bridle, feed, but I didn't think about that. All I knew was that I was getting another horse!

We brought Abby to her new home and she fit in perfectly. Abby was a beautiful chestnut mare that stood tall at 15.2 hands, which was a good size. My "family" was growing and I was still boarding them at the Foster's Ranch. But now I had three mouths to feed!

Right about this time I met another family by the same name of Foster. I had taught their daughter Merrit for a while when her trainer was on maternity leave. To help defray Abby's costs, they agreed to a partial lease. Dick was happy. Now the next items I seemed to need were a trailer and a vehicle to pull that trailer.

Dick found an '87 Ford 250 pickup truck, and he also researched and found a 3-horse trailer that was on sale.

Dick was an incredible support for my little hobby business. It was now becoming obvious (at least to me) that we needed our own horse property. Dick was living in what he considered his new dream house (this was not mine). I remember praying about what direction we should be going. I don't think Dick had the same prayer. However, in the end, he actually said, "Let's just look." Well, looking to me meant buying, because I never "window shop".

We found out an acquaintance from our Ridge Riders horse club was looking to sell their property in Covina. I went to look at this property, and I fell in love. Dick did not. The house was built in 1953, and was dated with a definite 70's look. Dick's dream house where we were living at the time was only a few years old and very modern.

This horse property was on an acre that went uphill. On the hill above the house were a beautiful well-built 4-stall barn and tack room that sat in the middle of the arena. The next level held four pipe corrals and the next level was a grassy hillside. I was in heaven. Dick wasn't quite there yet. He suggested that we continue to look around at what was available, so that's what we did.

We ended up looking at several properties, but none had what was necessary. They either had a great house with a poor horse facility (or none at all), or a house that needed a lot of work, but had a great horse facility. So back we came to the Covina house, which had both.

Another benefit to this house was that we weren't using a realtor, which would save both parties a lot of money. No one was in a hurry, so we could sell Dick's "dream" home and then proceed with this wonderful horse property.

To my delight, Dick finally gave in. The sale went smoothly, and in January 2000, in the pouring rain, we were able to move in. I was beside myself happy. Dick wasn't so sure.

My original idea was to have three horses in the barn in the winter. Then in the summer, keep them in the pipe corrals. That never happened. I filled every stall eventually. Some were horses I boarded for friends; others my own—eight in all.

We hadn't been in the house but three weeks when Joey (the hay delivery guy) came to deliver hay and feed. He opened the gate without me knowing he was there, and all three horses were in the arena. I heard hoofs on the driveway (which I should not have been hearing), so I ran out to see what was happening.

Abby and Rusty had escaped, and Knothead was coming

down the driveway at full speed. I stepped forward and called his name—I did not step in front of him (contrary to popular belief) because I knew better. Anyway, his chest hit mine and I went flying. I fell on my back and hit my head. Knothead went sailing out into the street. I think I lost consciousness.

Our Goddaughter, Tara, was living with us at the time and called 911. Joey the hay guy, saw what had happened and ran over to see how I was. It was still a little blurry, but I remember the paramedics asking me where I lived. I said, "San Dimas". Well, I did live there, three weeks ago. Then he asked me who the President was and I think I told him Jimmy Carter (Wrong! This happened in 2000). I'm guessing the paramedics determined that I wasn't quite right and needed medical attention. This was when they made the decision to airlift me to the Harbor UCLA Medical Center.

In the meantime, my parents were scheduled to arrive at any time that day for their first visit to our new abode. They were bringing my niece, Malia, who I had asked to speak at my P.E. classes on eating disorders that afternoon. My mother thought we (I) was nuts to leave Dick's dream house, even though she had a horse as a teenager and knew this house would be much more efficient. Because my parents didn't know the area, they ended up driving right past our house when the ambulance was in the driveway. They both saw the ambulance but quickly determined that it couldn't be our new home.

Our house was on a loop with one entrance, and when they got to the end and came back around in front, my mother screamed at my dad, "Stop the car! Those are Marcia's feet in that ambulance!" It's a good thing I was barefoot when I came running out of the house, or they may never have seen me!

My parents pulled up and ran over to the ambulance. I "instructed" them to take Malia to the school so she could give her talk to my classes. I assured them that I would be okay. I really don't remember a thing. This was recounted to me long after.

I was driven to the middle of a local baseball field where they loaded me into a helicopter. My head was securely stabilized so that I could not turn and look anywhere but straight up. I remember seeing the people hovering over me and talking like I wasn't there. Upon landing, I was surrounded by kind faces of several of the doctors.

Back at home, poor Tara had the unpleasant duty of calling my husband—who was the poster child for worry—

and explain to him how Knothead had run me over, and that I had to be airlifted to Harbor UCLA. I can't imagine getting a call like that, but Dick was a trooper. He took it pretty well.

Of course, by now the word was out. Marcia was run over by a horse! It might have been funny had it not been so serious and painful. An interesting thing happened, though, when my parents took Malia to the school. They had to explain to my students why I wasn't there and what had happened to me. I found out later that the whole school had prayed for me. What an honor that was to hear. To this day, I believe that God heard their prayers and He answered every one of them.

When all was said and done, the tests were clear, but I ended up having to have a few stitches in my elbow. The doctors were quite surprised after all that had happened that it wasn't worse.

As I look back on it now, I know this was another part of my life where God protected me. My job on this earth was not finished yet. And you animals lovers will be happy to know that Knothead was not injured at all.

CHAPTER 13

Rambo, etc...

As I shared before, we moved to *my* dream one-acre "ranchette" (not Dick's) in January 2000. I had big plans for this little piece of heaven and caring for my three horses. I knew God was going to move mountains. The acre was in layers; from the street, there was an uphill, half circle driveway to the house. Then further up a side driveway was the arena. In the middle of the arena was a four-stall barn and tack room. Continuing uphill from the arena to the second level were four pipe corrals that were shaded by a massive 100-year-old oak tree. From here you could walk up the hill (on steps that Dick put in) to a three-part chicken coop. Dick and our friend Daniel built this coop for me for Mother's Day one year. I eventually filled every stall, corral, coop, and cage with all types of animals.

One day some friends came to visit and told me I needed

to get a pig. Dick responded, "Over my dead body." But, thankfully, we didn't have to wait that long. I ended up getting three pigs—Munchie, George, and Gracie. I'll share more about them later.

The following week, our friend showed up with a pair of what were supposed to be pygmy goats (not very big). I called the girl goat Bambi and the little boy goat Rambo. They were only about eight weeks old and incredibly cute, and neither had been dehorned.

Sadly, Bambi crossed over the "Rainbow Bridge" three days later. I think she came to us very sick, and I was so new at being a goat owner, I didn't recognize her condition. Now it's certainly not funny that she died, but how does one get rid of a dead 25-pound goat? Well, the day she died happened to be "trash" day. We had a big dumpster for manure removal, but it had already been picked up. So my friend Dale, who was as crazy as me, said she had an idea.

We unceremoniously "bagged" Bambi and put her in the back of Dale's car. Then Dale took off and drove ahead of the trash truck on its route. She found a dumpster that hadn't been picked up yet, so Dale stopped and gave Bambi a quick "burial at dumpster." Problem solved, right? Not so fast…

We still had Rambo, who was now all alone. Goats are

herd animals and they need to have a herd. Since Bambi had left him alone, I then became his herd. He followed me everywhere. Remember, he had not yet been dehorned (a mistake, for sure, but who knew?), and Rambo began to grow, as did his horns. Every time the farrier came to shoe the horses, I had him trim Rambo's horns, which was a feat in itself.

Rambo wasn't supposed to be growing, remember? He was a pygmy. Well, Rammy, as I called him, finished out at a healthy 100 pounds, and trimming his horns became a bit of a battle. It was always a challenge, but one I would not let him win. I also learned to trim his feet. I did this by tying him to a fence and leaning my body against him. Eventually, Rammy learned to be somewhat obedient by the "spoken word", if it was loud enough.

Before Rammy got too big, he would always sit in the front seat of my truck with me when I hauled the horses to the arenas where I would teach my students. They all loved my goat. He also rode with me when I would drive my rig through the only fast food place where my truck and trailer could pull up to the drive-thru window. The owners always got a kick out of seeing Rammy sitting up front with me and would send French fries out for him. Contrary to popular belief, goats don't eat everything! Rammy was very particular about his fries.

This one day, during a lunchtime rush, Rammy and I pulled up to the window, and a man came over to the car looking very confused. "I've had a couple of beers and I want to make sure I'm not seeing things," he slurred. "Is that a goat in the front seat with you eating French fries?" I laughed pretty hard and assured him that it was indeed a goat and he wasn't seeing things. Rammy's drive-thru days ended when he got older and grew too big to sit in the truck. But he was always waiting at the gate for my return when lessons were over. We sure had fun while it lasted.

Rammy was my buddy and I loved him. When Dick and I made our move to Sparks, Nevada in 2013, we took him over to live with our wonderful neighbors as I didn't think he could withstand the cold winters in Sparks. Our neighbors had sheep that Rammy loved, and he eventually became the "king of the herd". He lived there happily until the early fall of 2016. He was 16 years old when he died, which is pretty good for an ol' goat.

Rambo was the first of many critters we had at the farm. As I recall, the next animal was Munchie, the pig I mentioned earlier. Munchie was a large, black pot-bellied pig. The principal at the school where I taught had a granddaughter who was one of my riding students. She needed to find a good home for Munchie and, of course, I already had a reputation of taking in homeless animals. So off I went to retrieve my new animal.

For whatever reason, I thought it a good idea to pick Munchie up in my minivan. What was I thinking? I'm not exactly sure, except that the van was lower than my truck, and I thought it would be easier on us both. It was an interesting sight to see—"encouraging" a 100-pound pig to walk the plank into the rear of the van. Needless to say, Munchie was thrilled to finally arrive at his new home, darting out the back of the van as fast as his chubby legs could run. This pig was only around about a year before he became ill and died. It was always so sad whenever we would lose a farm friend.

Not long after, I heard about someone in Whittier who had a litter of pot-bellied pigs. My friend Jessica and I drove down in her truck and picked out a male "pink" piglet, and a black female with a white stripe around her neck. As we drove home, I looked back at them and said, "George and Gracie." Now, most young people would not know who George and Gracie were (married comedy act, George Burns and Gracie Allen, from the 30s-50s), but I thought they were the perfect names.

They both grew to be great pigs and very friendly too. When the kids came over, they loved to spend time in their pens, brushing them, as well as feeding them. We tried bathing them once but decided it wasn't a good idea. Pigs are called pigs for a reason, so they stayed dirty. George was the friendliest out of the bunch. The kids loved to walk him around the neighborhood in his little blue harness and leash. It was quite a sight. But, as George grew bigger, he became a little more stubborn and I think somewhat lazy. So the kids pretty much left him alone after that.

Several times I was asked if I would bring some of my farm animals to a church or to a school. This would give the kids a chance to see what farm-living was all about, and have some interaction with them—petting them and getting to know them. The list of animals I brought was pretty long: Rusty the pony, Rambo (until he got ornery), then I would bring one of the twin goats I had acquired from the Knott's Berry Farm breeding program. I would also bring Lucy Goosie, Glenda the turkey, a no-name Mallard duck, a rabbit, and a chicken or a rooster—not sure which.

It was quite a production, and to watch us load them

all was hysterical. I usually had two or three of my older students assist me, which I was grateful to have them. Getting Rusty in my four-horse trailer was easy. In fact, that was the only easy part. We would have to catch each bird and put them in a cage. Many feathers were lost in the process. The rabbit was relatively easy and you were lucky if he or she didn't pee on you. This happened all too often, so the kids would draw lots as to who would secure a bunny. We would then load the cages onto the manure wagon, which had to be pulled with our golf cart.

Down the hill and around the barn we'd go, then down our long driveway to the street where my truck and trailer were parked. The next animal to load was George the pig. First, we had to "lead" him down the driveway…well maybe "pull" is a better word. It took much coaxing with treats but we finally got him to the trailer. Then the three of us had to lift him up. He weighed about 80 pounds. After a fair amount of squealing on George's part, we finally got him inside and he would run over to his corner. Then we loaded the cages, secure everyone and off we'd go.

The teens that helped me were fabulous! I loved watching them interact with the kids as well as the adults. They had learned so much from being with the animals and learning about them. It was extremely satisfying to me to see these kids impart their knowledge of the animals that they were in charge of.

After we finished our "educational show", we had to reverse the process—back into their cages and into the trailer. Again, Rusty was so easy, he could load himself. Then there was George. Up he went into the trailer squealing and running into his corner. The kids loved it. It was part of the "show". Once we got home it was fairly easy. Out came the cages onto the manure wagon. When we lifted George out, he would scamper up the driveway. He knew he was home and that he'd be getting a treat. Rusty unloaded himself and walked up the driveway to his pen. A good time was had by all. As a big "thank you", I would always take my helpers to lunch afterward.

There were more animals than I can count that stayed at the farm. I rescued many birds that people had found as lost babies. The majority of them were Mallard ducks, and I raised most of them until they were old enough to live on their own. Then I would release them on the creek that was at the end of my street, called Walnut Creek.

One morning, I heard from a dear friend of mine. We all called her Auntie June. She was quite the character. Auntie

June was a very strong woman who spoke her mind. She called to tell me there was a young goose in her front yard and would I please come get it! So like a good neighbor, I loaded a cage in my minivan and went off to collect who we would soon refer to as Lucy. Lucy Goosie. She wasn't but maybe six months old. I did some research and found out that Lucy was a Toulouse Goose. Over the next several months, Lucy and I spent a lot of time together and eventually she became very tame.

CHAPTER 14

It's All In The Name

At last "The Farm" was taking form with various animals and horses. I would teach lessons in the arena that surrounded my barn. This arena only worked with beginners who would walk and trot. I soon started loading the horses in my trailer and taking them Ridge Riders Park, which was owned by a club of the same name where Dick and I were members. My friend Kash Grimes lived on the property and also gave lessons. She was always sweet and so encouraging to me, and she accepted me for what I really was—an instructor for beginner riders. Many of the other trainers looked down on me. In their opinion, I wasn't a real trainer, and they didn't have many kind things to say. However, I didn't really care. I was doing what I loved—working with horses and children!

God placed Kash in my life at a time when I needed her the most. Kash educated me in every aspect of teaching, showing, and also how to work with horses. I listened intently and soaked in her every word. I was so grateful for her patient heart and her loyal friendship.

Another woman that I was so grateful for was DeAnn, my artist friend with many talents. DeAnn was the one who encouraged me to name "The Farm". After much thought and elimination of other names, and because I loved horses and birds, the farm was finally christened with the perfect, proper name—Horse Feather Farm. DeAnn also suggested that I have a logo, and because of her incredible artistic talent, she came up with a unique and fitting one for Horse Feather Farm. She drew a horseshoe right side up with the name Horse Feather Farm at the top and a feather running through the center. This graphic turned out to be the perfect design for the business cards that another friend (Jayne) had suggested I have made and which she designed. The end results were amazing, with the red and tan logo in the upper right corner, contact information, and what our facility did below. Also, if you looked closely in the background on the card, you could see a faint photo of me with Rusty (my Pony) who is leaning over and kissing me. Eventually, Dick had my logo printed on a magnetic sign that I was able to put on my trailer and the doors of my truck. I was officially in business!

That first summer at the farm, in 2000, I decided to try my hand at a one-week day camp. After all, I was fairly knowledgeable in day camps (after spending much of my youth being involved in them), so why not do this at the farm? The first camp I had was called "horsey" camp and I enlisted three of my teenage helpers to be counselors—Erin, Bonnie, and Becca. There were about 8-10 "campers" in attendance, and though I don't recall much about that first week, it was definitely the beginning of something amazing.

The next summer (2001), I conducted four camps. Two were "farm" camps and two were "horsey" camps. Once again, my friend Jayne made colorful registration forms for these camps and she also suggested that I have T-shirts made with our logo. That year we had bright blue ones made for students and counselors. On the back of the counselors' shirts, it said "Staff" which they seemed proud to wear. The students' shirts had either horsey camp or farm camp written on the back, depending on which camp they attended.

Every year thereafter we had a different color T-shirt made: dark green 2002, red 2003, orange 2004, yellow 2005, purple 2006, turquoise 2007, lime green 2008, bright blue (again) 2009. In 2010, my friend Linda, whose twin daughters took lessons from me, made a suggestion to do tie-dyed shirts. Linda was very creative with crafts and needlework and she volunteered to "help". Ha! Help indeed! She ending up doing the whole process and I was so grateful. In 2010 and 2011, the T-shirts were multicolored, and everyone had a great time creating their own color theme.

My little "Horse Feather Farm" was turning into such a huge success, with five to six camps all summer long and me teaching riding lessons on the weekends.

By the time 2010 came around, I was growing a little weary. I loved so much putting on these camps every year, but I felt my ideas were somewhat stale and I wasn't sure what to do. I was pretty sure that God didn't want me retiring just yet, and I truly believed that He brought Linda into my life to lend a hand. She was like a breath of fresh air—full of energy and new ideas. What a difference she made in my life. We had such a fun planning and working together. She was definitely a Godsend.

CHAPTER 15

My Horse Feather Farm Staff

Each year I chose my "counselors" from a list of my older riding students. I didn't just ask anyone—I was very selective. I had to be. And I prayed about it too, which was why it took a great deal of thought and consideration. Counselors where chosen on their personality, patience, knowledge, maturity, dependability, as well as their ability to teach. Safety was always my biggest concern.

I developed a leadership program that required each counselor to attend, which was usually a one or two-day training. During this time, we went over safety, teamwork skills, problem-solving, and sharing all our own ideas. In many ways, it felt as if I were teaching them not only how to be great camp counselors, but also life skills that they could put to use later in life—like how to get along with coworkers, how to deal with conflict, how to solve problems, how to be safe, how to be responsible and dependable, etc.

During the training, these individuals were taught to work a problem out first with a coworker or camper before they deferred it to me. We would use different scenarios and role-play situations. It was also mandatory that all counselors attend the counselor meeting every morning before camp started so that we could go over the day's activities. If there were any camper challenges during the day, we would go over each one and discuss a possible solution. This was always helpful to everyone.

Over the course of each summer, I enjoyed so much watching each of these young people learn, stretch and grow into someone they might not have had a chance to be. I felt so blessed to see lifelong friendships form, not only with each other but with me as well. It was these kids who made HFF work. They made it successful. I would watch as teenagers who didn't think they could work with little children, blossom and learn and, by the end of camp, even love the kids they had taught—and they enjoyed doing it, too.

After the first few years, I instituted a CIT (Counselor in Training) program. This was where I could bring in some of my younger students to start learning how to be counselors. Each CIT would be paired with a "seasoned" counselor for their first year so they would know how to do the job, which also helped them to feel more comfortable when camp started.

Dates for summer camps were scheduled every January when I would go over my calendar for the year. I would send out registration forms to all the campers who had previously attended camp, and also send out contracts to all possible counselors and CITs. This system seemed to work best for me. The students could pick the dates they wanted to volunteer, and then discuss it with their parents before they made a commitment to come onboard. During our training workshops, we would talk extensively about what it meant to make a commitment. Then when the kids had the opportunity to put this into action, it gave me a great sense of pride to know that they all had paid attention and actually learned a great life's lesson as well.

During "horsey camp" there were two counselors and one CIT. They were assigned a team of four campers and were in charge of one horse. I would talk to them about teamwork, commitment, and responsibility, and to always remember to put your teammate and campers first, above all else. I would often use scenarios to make a point. "Let's say you get up one morning and you don't feel like coming to camp? Who does this affect and reflect on?"

Then I would explain: "First and foremost, it would affect the campers who needed and expected both of their counselors. But one chose not to show. And what about your partner?" I asked. "If one doesn't show, the other would be responsible for, not only their work but the work of their partner as well! How would this make you feel if it were you?" I asked again, trying to make a point. Then I ended the lesson with, "So get up! Get dressed! And get yourself to camp!" And they always did. Although there were days when some would stagger in like they had just rolled out of bed (which, of course, they did) but at least they showed up, and on time, too! We also had several lessons and conversations on attitude.

Attitude was everything. It was summer and it was hot—a fact that no one could change. So I told them to "Get over it and smile. Show them your grit. Be determined to give these kids a great camp and a memory that will last them a lifetime." I am proud to say that these kids never let me down.

In 2002, I introduced a "theme" for each summer. I called

them my Character Themes. It was important for us to be able to have a starting point and one that we would stick to throughout the length of the camp. The "theme" titles we used were:

2002 – Be Accountable

2003 – Attitude of Gratitude

2004 – Humble Winner/Gracious Loser (my fav!)

2005 – Honesty is the Best Policy

2006 – Giving — Going the Extra Mile

2007 – Giveaway — Sharing is Caring

2008 – Leave a Place/Person Better Than You Found Them

2009 – Remember to Finish What You Begin

2010 – Do the Right Thing — Do Things Right

2011 – Pay it Forward

CHAPTER 16

A Day at "Farm Camp"

Farm Camp started every morning at 8:00am sharp with a counselors' meeting. By the end of the week, the sharpness and reality of the 8:00am arrival wore off, as they dragged themselves through the front door, not looking as bright-eyed and alert as had Monday morning.

Our meeting started with the day's activities. We would go over the assigned team's rotation, discussed any challenges, and then we would all pray together giving our day and our safety to the Lord. Not everyone had a faith. However, they knew I based my faith and trust in God, so they all participated. I was hoping that some of my faith would wear off on them. Plus, I felt it was important to cover our day's activities in prayer.

After the meeting, each team would make sure that their

"red" cups were all washed, dried and put in their team box. Each camper and counselor had a "red" cup with their name on it for drinks. Everyone was responsible for their own cup for the entire week. (I explained this at our orientation meeting and basically threatened them with their lives to keep track of their cup.) If they could do this for the entire week, they would be illegible for a prize—usually candy or something similar. This system worked well as we had very few lost cups—and campers!

There was one team in charge of filling the lemonade and water jugs, and then putting them on the table outside. Also, this team was responsible for making sure these jugs made it into the back of the camp van at lunchtime, so the campers could refill their cups. The assigned team knew their job and did it well. Every so often, when I felt the counselors were "wandering," I would whisper in their ear, "On task." This reminder brought them right back to work. They were such great kids—all of them. However, they were still kids and they needed to be supervised—hence, the bunny incident. Let me explain.

One summer, two of the counselors (maybe three, though only two were willing to fess up) thought it would be fun to "introduce" one of the boy bunnies to the three girl bunnies I purposely had in separate cages. Unbeknownst to me, three weeks later, there were three litters of seven bunnies each! Mind you, this is on top of the 15 bunnies I had already! I was livid, to say the least. We had a meeting where two of the counselors admitted that they had played a part in this romantic fiasco.

There was no way I was keeping all of these bunnies, and also there had to be some sort of reprimand for these playful counselors. So I came up with a plan. The two culprits had to find homes for all 21 baby bunnies or explain to their parents why they had to bring them home. I think one of the counselors ended up taking a couple of them home, but the rest of them all found homes. I thought for sure I'd end up getting some of them back when the kids grew tired of them, but I never did. God has a reason for everything. It was a good lesson to teach these kids on being responsible for animals' lives. God also has a sense of humor—21 baby bunnies! Oh my! Thankful to Him that He made it work. Now back to the business of camp.

First thing in the morning, campers would spend time at their tables doing simple crafts and getting to know each other until everyone arrived. Each camper and counselor wore a name tag around their neck so they were easy to see. At the counselor meetings, I would hand out a sheet of smiley stickers to each counselor to be used as rewards for the campers who would, naturally and without thought, go above and beyond what was expected. Campers would earn a sticker whenever the counselor saw someone being kind to another, sharing, helping, stepping out of their comfort zone, being brave and trying something new—i.e. touching a rooster or a fat, pot-bellied pig for the first time could be frightening.

Stickers were given with love and praise and were placed on the back of the camper's name tag. Needless to say, there were always those kids who would only do something nice when someone was watching, but they rarely received a sticker. We called them "suck ups". And we had several over the years. Linda and I would also give out stickers to the counselors for their work well done. We praised them for good teamwork, working out problems, helping another team with their chores, etc. It was a great tool to encourage and to bring attention to their kindness.

After "table time" and everyone had arrived, we filed through the house out to the circular driveway, where we all assembled in a semi-circle facing the front door. Above the door was the American flag. Then I asked one of the volunteers to lead us in the Pledge of Allegiance and say a prayer after. Then the volunteer would explain the theme for the day. Whoever stepped forward was rewarded with a sticker for being so brave. By the end of the week, even the younger kids were volunteering.

After the theme was explained, everyone was dismissed; half would go back to their tables and work on their miniature farms and the other half would go to the barn to be with the animals.

At Farm Camp, one animal or feathered friend would be selected to learn more about and how to take care of them. Depending on which animal was chosen, there would be a lesson on cleaning—their pen, stall, aviary, or chicken coop.

When "Pig Day" came, I always made sure the "pig lady" was available to assist us. She would come and show the campers how to trim the pig's hooves and cut their teeth back. This process was fascinating to watch. However, my pigs, George and Gracie, were not always willing participants in this process. Because of the horrendous noise that George and Gracie made, I had to warn the neighbors when the "pig lady" was coming so that when the neighbors heard the bloodcurdling screams, they would know we weren't getting them ready to roast. These pigs of mine had a set of lungs on them that far out measured any baby I knew.

When we had "Horsey Day", I always made sure to schedule my farrier (that's a person who shoes horses for all you lay people). Being a farrier is not as popular today as back when horses were one of the only forms of transportation. A farrier is now usually applied specifically to a blacksmith who specializes in shoeing horses—a skill that requires not only the ability to shape and fit horseshoes, but also the ability to clean, trim, balance and shape a horse's hooves.

I had several farriers over the years who were all wonderful and patient with the kids, and taking the extra time to explain each tool and what it did. If I noticed any camper not paying attention and goofing off (which they did often), I told them there would be a test at the end of the week so they'd better be listening. Of course, there was never a test, but they sure did listen better!

Then there was "Goat Day". This day was always very interesting, not because it was anything special, but because of the goats. Rambo, my big ol' goat, was not the friendliest animal. Plus, he had big horns, which actually scared many people away. He usually spent the morning in a closed stall and would complain openly about his confinement.

I also had another goat named Becky (it was Becca first, but I changed her name). Becky was a small pygmy goat that someone had given to me. A few years back, I had been known to rescue anything that breathed, so people were always dropping off animals for me to rescue. Becky's original owners had bought her to live on their hillside and to keep it clear. However, after the purchase, they realized that their home was not zoned for goats, which led me to believe that they never looked at the actual CC&R's before they brought her home, and the neighbors complained.

My friend Deanna (owner of San Dimas Grain Co.) would always call me with homeless animal requests. "Will you take this goat?" She asked one day. "Of course I will," I told her. What's one more animal? Good news for me though. Becky turned out to be a lot friendlier than Rambo. But then again, anything was friendlier than Rambo. I loved him and he put up with my loving him.

For the campers who participated in "Goat Day", one of the things I would demonstrate was how to keep the goat's hooves trimmed. Believe it or not, Rambo was the best subject for this demonstration. I had to tie him closely and tightly to the pipe corral fence. Then I proceeded to pick up his hoof like a farrier would do for a horse (good thing I paid attention!). For tools, I would use a very sharp garden trimmer to do the job. Rambo was a large goat, but he kicked like a pony. He was probably one of the main reasons my arms were so strong back then because I held on tight so he wouldn't get away. Then after I was through and the campers were satisfied, Rambo would be looking for his treat, which he knew was always waiting in my pocket.

Of course "Horse Day" was always the most popular day. Each team was assigned a horse that they would all take care of for the day. I always had to chuckle at the campers who professed to be die-hard horse lovers. When it came time to clean the stalls (my favorite chore!), they would hold their noses, and say, "Yucky, I can't possibly do this!" My response was, "If you love horses, you have to love all that goes with a horse." Clean up was part of the job.

I would also stress many times over that they were part of a team, and as part of a team, they needed to help. The counselors were great at encouraging the campers and showing them that they could overcome their doubts, fears and unpleasant duties, and accomplish the task. The counselors would also remind the kids that after they had cleaned up the stalls, they would then be able to do their most preferred chore, which was grooming the horse.

This was a lesson in itself as they would learn the various tools that were needed to brush the horse. Some of these kids were no taller than the horse's belly, which meant they spent much of the time grooming their legs. But they all had fun until they had to clean the horse's hooves. Once again, "Yucky" and "Gross" could be heard throughout the barn.

The best part was yet to come when each camper would be given the opportunity to ride this beautiful animal. This was another one of my own personal favorite days. Most of the campers who came to "Farm Camp" had never been exposed to a horse before. Their faces said it all, as their eyes lit up and their smiles went from ear to ear in awe and wonder. It was pure joy whenever these kids mounted and rode this large 1000 pound beast. For me, this moment was more valuable and worth far more money than anything I would ever make at this farm (which really wasn't much at all!) My counselors and I made a great team and the campers continuously reaped the benefits year after year of our combined skills. God had blessed us greatly.

"Bird Day" was no doubt the most hilarious. I had an aviary with several cockatiels, a bunch of parakeets and two button quail. Unfortunately, the quail would duke it out and would eventually kill each other—survival of the "fittest", but in this case, neither was "fit" enough!

The most fun was in the chicken and duck coop and trying to catch these birds. It was hysterical. The ducks had their makeshift "ponds" (blue plastic swimming pools) and many times the counselors had to run through the ponds to catch them. Feathers would fly everywhere and these ducks quacked very loud in their attempt to get away. Again, the counselors stepped up and were real troopers.

The campers seemed to enjoy collecting eggs the best. When Glenda the turkey and Lucie Goosie were around, everybody got into the act. Collecting eggs was not only challenging, but also very interesting as some of the chickens laid different colors of eggs—not just white but light green, light blue and brown. This fascinated the campers.

After collecting several dozen, they would weigh them on Dick's ancient egg scale that he had brought back from a New England dairy farm. And afterward, the kids had to crack them open just to see if the white ones were any different inside than the colored ones. Imagine their surprise when they realized all the eggs were the same! This was a life lesson I shared with them often. Just like people with different skin color—on the outside, they all look different, but inside our blood runs red. We all bleed the same! Isn't that just like our God?

Every Wednesday of Farm Camp was "Creek Day", which meant picking berries. After "table time" and the flag ceremony, the campers were instructed to put on water shoes or old sneakers and gather into teams. Each counselor was given enough plastic sandwich bags for their team. Then each team would walk to the end of the street where Walnut Creek gently flowed. After passing through the gate and down a short path, we found the creek, which was lined with blackberries ripe for the picking—on the opposite side of the creek!

Now in order to get these juicy berries, one would have to cross the creek. You would have thought we were asking these kids to cross the Rio Grande! Who knew what evil fish and or insect lurked in the depths of these flowing waters? We were talking about two feet—at the most. Once again, my "rock" of counselors would show their kindness and patience as they encouraged and guided these kids to step out in faith and into the water and cross over. Some of the counselors had to step out and leave their comfort zone to help these kids overcome their fears, and I was very proud of them.

Knowing that there would be a prize for the team with

the most berries was also encouraging and it would help many of the campers to want to complete the task. After all the berries had been poured into a team bag and "judged", we then would hike back to the house and to camp where they would hose off and dry out. Then we would proceed to take turns in the kitchen and make miniature blackberry pies for the campers to take home. We also made applesauce.

Thursday mornings each team would take turns in the kitchen peeling apples on an old-fashioned apple peeler—the kind where you would turn the handle and the apple would be cored and peeled. The kids were fascinated by this unique device. Then I would cook the apples down and add a little sugar, and we all would enjoy the warm homemade applesauce before they left for home. I wanted very much for these children to experience what it might be like living on a farm, taking care of animals, and tasting some real farm cooking.

As I mentioned before, we enjoyed many crafts at Farm Camp. But the favorite was when each camper got to build their own model farm. They were each given a 1½ x 1½ Masonite board and a package of plastic animals to use in the construction of their farms. All year I would save paper towel rolls (made great silos), green plastic fruit baskets and Popsicle sticks (for fencing), blue cellophane paper (for ponds), Astroturf (for grass), and all kinds of other odds and ends. Dick would graciously assemble all the necessary items needed: plywood bases, and different sizes and pieces of wood. He played a very large role in many of my "farm" ideas, rarely complaining and always willing to lend a hand—and I cannot thank him enough.

Each day, the campers were given time to work on their farms. I so enjoyed watching them help each other, giving each other ideas and sharing and trading their supplies. At the end of the week, they were so proud to show their parents what they had designed and built. A lifetime treasure for sure!

When lunchtime came around, the campers would pick out a spot on the front lawn to eat, and then they would all play games until it was time to go home. On the last day of camp, we would have a water balloon toss and enjoy popsicles. When I saw the mess in the front yard that the broken water balloons had made, I knew I didn't want to be the one picking them all up. So I created a contest. Whoever collected the most broken balloons would get a prize! It was genius! Kid power—gotta love it!

On the very last day of camp we would have an "Awards

Ceremony". The day before, at the counselor meeting, I would hand out 3 x 5 cards to each of the counselors. They were asked to write something positive and complimentary about each of the campers (i.e. most friendly, most helpful, most cheerful, most creative"etc.), and the counselors were always willing to participate as they enjoyed coming up with different ways to award these kids.

At the ceremony, the counselors would then present a ribbon to the camper and explain to them why they chose this particular compliment that described this particular camper. It was such a small thing, but the campers felt so special. Every year our ribbons would match the shirts we wore that year (and yes, we even had a tie-dyed ribbon made).

I loved to watch the counselors when they would award the "character" ribbons, for many of them had to step way out of their comfort zone in order to fulfill this task. It wasn't always easy because they knew they would literally have to make up something good to say about some of these kids who were challenging. It was especially important because on the last day of horsey camp all the moms, dads, aunts and uncles were in the audience! But once again, my counselors did not disappoint. Of course, they had no choice with the camp director making eye contact and silently praying to "Please, be kind." I was so proud of them all.

There were also 1st through 6th place ribbons given out to the team and individuals with the most stickers on their name tags, as well as a small, engraved trophy with a horse on it that would go to "Best All-Around Camper", which the counselors would vote on every year. Sometimes a simple gesture of appreciation would go farther than words could ever say.

After I closed the farm, I found one of these trophies tucked away in a closet. So I kept it for myself as a reminder of those days that were so special to so many. Now, I certainly was not the most outstanding camper—far from it, in fact. Maybe I should have the engraving changed to the "Oldest Camper in History"! If nothing else, it would certainly make for some great conversation.

CHAPTER 17

A Day at "Horsey Camp"

If I had enough counselors, I could usually handle up to 30 campers for Farm Camp. Horse Camps had to be limited. We used four horses (which made sense, as I only had a 4-horse trailer). I would then assign two counselors (or a counselor and a CIT) to four campers. This team was placed with a horse that could handle the camper's abilities. It literally would take me hours to form these teams, as I wanted to be sure to have counselors that worked well together and could manage the age group of their campers.

Needless to say, safety was always first and foremost in my mind. Dick taught me how to teach the kids about the "circle of safety"—walk around the truck and the trailer to see if everything was where it should be before proceeding.

Horsey Camp began much like Farm Camp. We had our table time, flag ceremony and then each team went up the hill to take care of their assigned steed. On the first day, the campers would meet their horse. Most of them were elated, but some of the younger ones were a little hesitant. To a small 8-year-old, these 1000 pounds animals looked gigantic!

The staff would use this first morning to go over safety, impressing upon these eager young cowboys and cowgirls the dangers of being around such a large, intimidating beast. After their safety lesson, there was a demonstration as to how to groom them. Then it was on to everyone's favorite chore...stall cleaning. Some teams were lucky if they had the horse that only pooped in one spot. I believe that was Kali. She made the campers stall-cleaning so much easier. If the team was unfortunate enough to be paired with Sparkle, she seemed to delight in having her manure all over her stall. Then there were horses like Rusty, who would pull his hay out of the feeder and spread it everywhere.

At the end of chore time, we had "inspection". I always loved Horsey Camp because my stalls and corrals (and horses) were spotless! On occasion, the stalls of the horses who weren't participating in the week's camp were cleaned out too, which gave the teams extra smiley stickers. I delighted in camper labor!

There were some parents who would send their child to camp just to "cure" their love for horses. The parents were under the mistaken belief that if their dainty, little girl had to shovel manure she would never want a horse of her own. However, this misconception backfired every time. These girlie-girls couldn't get enough of doing all the things that involved caring for a horse.

After "inspection", we would have our sticker meeting (strange how the kids made getting a sticker of the utmost importance). There was a poster with each campers name on it. Each child would call out how many smiley face stickers they had and we would match those stickers next to their names. This was also done for teams. It turned out to be a great way to encourage these kids and their teams to work harder. We were careful to note if there was a child who didn't have many stickers and look for ways to praise them for doing something positive. Our motto was always: "No camper left behind."

Afterward, we would load the horses and campers for our ride to Ridge Riders Park. I was blessed to have moms like Linda and young adults like Erin who would help drive to the arenas in our 12-passenger van and the minivan. Every camper had an assigned car, truck or van and they loaded with precision.

Upon arrival, everyone had an assigned duty. Once the horses were unloaded and given a hay bag, it was time for lunch. We stressed the importance that the horses were always taken care of first. When we finished lunch, the team would help tack up their team horse. Usually, the counselors did most of the saddling and bridling or we would have been there much longer and never have the chance to ride.

Each counselor would take her team and horse in the assigned arena and would work on basic riding skills. My counselors were so amazing and so attentive to their campers. They would either keep the horse on a lead line or walk right next to the horse as the kids were on their mount. We would do half-hour intervals at which time I would blow a whistle and everyone, including counselors, would change stations. There were four stations in all: a "riding" station, a "game" station, "craft" station, and a "knowledge" station. This event went smoothly and would cover everything the camper would need by week's end.

Thursday of camp week seemed to always be the campers' favorite. It was finger painting day, which meant that each camper got to finger paint their horse! The rule was that each team had to come up with their own design. They loved smearing the gooey finger paint all over their subject and, for the most part, the horse would stand still and cooperate. The staff would judge their creations and there would be prizes for 1st through 4th place—which everyone usually received candy.

Then the campers would proceed to bathe their horse so they would be all clean and shinny for their "horse show" on Friday. This chore was particularly fun on a hot summer's day, and most of the kids were picked up in soaking wet clothes.

By the time Friday arrived, everyone was a pack of nerves. Their families and friends were coming to watch them show off their new found skills, and they knew they needed to be at their best.

The campers would spend their mornings practicing on the obstacle course that they had designed. Then after lunch their families would come, and each child would demonstrate the skills they had learned. After the festivities, we served lemonade and cookies to everyone, and then the families shared in our awards ceremony.

For these kids, it was the highlight of their week. By day's end, everyone went home—hot, tired, dirty, but very very happy!

I cannot end this chapter without giving God praise once again for how He handled my situation with the City. As you have read, the horse camps were all conducted at my home and at the Ridge Riders Arena from 2002-2009—four horse camps each summer, five days a week. But in the early spring of 2010, when my camps were filling up, the City decided that I would have to start paying to use the arenas, and what they were asking was completely out of my budget…not to mention unreasonable. I had been using this place for years, and all of a sudden I was supposed to start paying for it. The City wanted to charge $250 a day, which would have been around $5,000 by the end of summer! There was no way I could afford to do that, which meant that I was going to have to refund the campers their money, cancel camp, and disappoint a whole lot of children. The only thing I knew to do was pray and give it to God. So I did! And He answered.

I ended up approaching one of my counselor's parents, Paul and Ronda, whose daughter Bonnie had been with me for several summers. Paul and Ronda had built a beautiful equestrian estate called Rose Gables Ranch. I explained what was going on and they were so warm and gracious. They understood my dilemma, and they offered to let me conduct my horse camps at their ranch. We agreed on the amount of $600 for the summer. I was so relieved and so very grateful!

For me, those last few years were the most memorable years at Horse Feather Farm. God not only gave me an alternative place to hold my horse camps, He gave me the best… He always does!

CHAPTER 18

The Horseless Hayride

At one of the first farm camps, we discovered that there was a period of time that I needed to fill with some activity. After much thought, we came up with the "horseless hayride".

The Farm had a green electric golf cart that we would hitch to our manure trailer, a very stinky little two-wheeler. Daniel, the fellow who would help out with cleaning stalls and dumping the manure into our huge dumpster, would drive this contraption whenever it was needed, which made the job much easier and efficient. Daniel sort of came with the house when we bought it. He worked for the previous owner and kindly agreed to stay on and work for us. We felt extremely blessed as he knew the property so well. He was another Godsend.

Daniel not only cleaned out the stalls, he could do pretty

much anything, and he was always available to support us with things that needed doing. When we came up with a plan to fill the activity gap for the kids, the "horseless hayride" was born. This golf cart and trailer would enable us to give the campers an enjoyable ride between activities.

Daniel and I would spend the much needed time sweeping out the manure in the trailer and trying to clean it up as best we could (you can imagine the odor which seemed to linger for weeks). After it was swept, a small amount of hay was added (or we couldn't call it a "hayride"). Because our street was actually a circle, it made it easy to give these "rides" to the campers.

The cart would hold four to six kids, depending on their size. Then I would get behind the wheel and drive it in a big circle around the street. Some days everyone was given the chance to ride before the golf cart "horse" would lose power and stop. But there were other days when patience was needed because we had to wait for the cart to be recharged, which turned out to be a good lesson for these kids to learn. This simple, yet ingenious, activity turned out to be one of the most popular for the kids. Who knew?

CHAPTER 19

Horses God Provided

When I look back on these amazing years, I see how God provided every horse in my life. I owned some, borrowed some, and some I had leased, but every one of them was hand-picked by the Lord. I've already told you how I acquired Knothead, Rusty and Abby. The horse that came after was a beautiful paint named "Dox Montana Doll" aka Sparkle.

At the time, I had a young student named Bonnie whom I was teaching to ride on Abby. Her parents wanted to buy their daughter a horse but it couldn't be just any horse, as Bonnie was very tall and had long legs. The horse had to fit Bonnie's frame and Abby was the perfect size. However, if I sold them Abby I would be a horse short and would need to find another quickly. My friend Kash owned Sparkle but she was not a good match for Bonnie as Sparkle was not a very tall horse. I would have loved to buy Sparkle, but she was way out of my price range.

I didn't feel comfortable selling Abby because she had been given to me. (However, Dick would have had no problem at all!) How do you sell a *free* horse? What should I do? Abby was perfect for Bonnie and I knew this horse should be hers. I did the only thing I could do. I prayed. I left it in God's hands as to what I should do.

God answers prayers in many ways, and once again He did not disappoint. As it turned out, Bonnie's parents decided to buy Sparkle for me and I, in turn, gave Abby to Bonnie. WOW! Talk about being blessed! Kash who was an outstanding trainer, had trained Sparkle and she was a great horse. But even though Kash may have trained her well, she was still a paint. Paint horses are known for being stubborn, and Sparkle was no exception. I had one little girl who would go in the corner of the arena and cry after every lesson because she couldn't get Sparkle to move. Fast forward a few years: That same little girl went on to be a great team rider with Sparkle and won many ribbons. You couldn't force Sparkle—you had to ask her! Sparkle turned out to be a blessing for many of the students.

Then came Kali. In the spring of 2003, I was visiting a

stable in the next town over and I walked past a stall that had a beautiful gray Arabian inside. There was a sign on the feed bin saying she was for sale. Horses are for sale all the time, but it was the content of this sign that caught my eye. It said: "Kalendar Girl, 18 years old, for sale for $1000. This price includes an English saddle, Western saddle, bridles to match, winter blanket, saddle pads, etc. Call the number below."

My first thought, of course, was "What's wrong with this horse?" So I called the number and a gentleman answered. I asked him why he was selling her so cheap. He explained, "I gave my daughter six months to sell her before she went off to college. She left yesterday and hadn't sold her so I put the sign up today." What are the odds?

I also noticed on the stall card that we had the same Vet. I asked the man if he would give me permission to call the Vet and ask about the medical history of the horse. He agreed, so I called. The Vet told me she was a great horse and would be perfect for my program. Now it happened to be in June of that year, and I actually had the camp deposits and payments in the bank. So I had the $1000 I needed! After having one of my students try her out, I bought her! Kali would have easily sold and very quickly for that price.

What are the chances of me being there right after the man put up the for sale sign? I don't believe in coincidences. This was truly a gift from God!

I won't say a lot about every horse, but Kali was one of the favorites. I had always wanted to ride in a parade. Since I purchased her in June, the 4th of July was just around the corner. LaVerne, the town next to us, held a 4th of July parade every year. So I signed up. I also signed up one of my students named Katie. We had a blast washing the horses (she rode Rusty and I rode Kali), and decorating them with red, white and blue ribbons and glitter. I believe I even made an American flag out of glitter on Kali's behind. We were stylin'! Katie and I even practiced our "wave".

Kali turned out to be an amazing addition to our program. She taught many children and adults how to ride. When she seemed not to enjoy giving lessons any longer, I gave her to one of my students to love on her. Marisa had her for another four years and enjoyed riding Kali bareback all over the hills of West Covina. Kali passed away peacefully on September 5, 2012 in the loving arms of her owner Marisa. Kali was almost 30 years old.

In June 2003, the week after the first Horsey Camp, Knothead had severely injured his knee and fetlock (ankle) joints. When the Vet came to check him, I saw the look on his face—it wasn't good. I took Knothead to the local equine hospital located in the next town. After X-rays and a very thorough examination, it was determined that the best option for Knotty was to let him cross over the "Rainbow Bridge", which meant we had to put him down. That was one of the toughest days I ever had at HFF—saying goodbye to my very first horse. What a gift from God he had been for me. He taught not only me but many others as well, how to handle and to treat a horse.

I mourned for days, but then I had to get real. I was in a predicament. I had five more camps to go and I was short one horse! I prayed as I always do and gave it to the Lord. At the next Ridge Rider board meeting, I shared my dilemma. Most people were using their own horses so it would be difficult to borrow a horse for the summer, or at least the weeks when camp was in session.

One of the board members raised mini horses, but she had a small horse she said she'd be happy to lend me. This was when Pride entered our lives and spent the summer with us at HFF. God had answered my prayer again!

In 2003, my good friend Jessica asked me to board a horse in my barn. She would often times acquire a horse from the

Santa Anita racetrack. Then she would retrain it and put it up for sale. I really liked Jess. She also accepted me and taught me plenty. We both knew that it was God who had allowed our paths to cross and we felt blessed and grateful.

In 2003, Jess brought Jumby Bay to live in my barn. Even though I am much more of a Quarter horse lover, Jumby was a Thoroughbred, and she was the most beautiful animal I had ever laid eyes on. She was reddish bay (brown horse with black mane and tail) with no white on her anywhere.

Jumby had come from Santa Anita racetrack and had actually run her last race on October 23, 2003. Jess picked her up not too long after and brought her to me. Jumby had never been injured while racing, she just wasn't fast enough and she wasn't a very big Thoroughbred, only 15.3 hands.

Jess and I would ride the trails on Walnut Creek which was just down the street from me. There were many parts to the trail where you had to cross the creek. I would follow along behind Jess and Jumby would walk right through the water. Sometimes she needed a little encouraging, but Jumby would always go through. This Thoroughbred was only three years old and she was right off the track! I was amazed, but then again, Jess was an excellent rider.

Well as it happened, I ended up falling in love with

Jumby Bay, and bought her for $1000. Jess was kind enough to let me make $100 a month payments (remember I never had any money!) So now what? I have this three-year-old race horse, and I was not a horse "trainer". I knew enough to get by, but that's about all. I arranged with a real trainer friend (Karen) to give lessons on Jumby to Katie, one of my students. This way both horse and student could learn together! Jumby may not have been fast, but boy could she jump! This precious animal eventually became part of the riding and camp programs. She was a great asset to the farm.

Somewhere around 2004, another friend of mine teamed up with me to teach and to run the camps together. Her name was Pam and she brought much experience as well as extra horses for us to use. We had a great year and camp was full with many students and campers. Then to my disappointment, Pam decided to take over one of the local stables and she was no longer able to help at HFF. But we had many fun memories together.

The next horse to join our booming business was Angel, although she was far from anything that resembled an angel. In 2000, my friend DeAnn Foster bought nine-month-old Angel, for her 12-year-old daughter Merrit. Angel was a P.O.A. (Pony of America). That's a breed that started in the mid-1950s. Someone decided to cross a Shetland pony stallion with an appaloosa mare—and the breed was born. Rusty was also a P.O.A.

Angel came with the registered name of Suncrest's Buttercup, but Merrit changed it to Strawberry Angel. To us she was Angel. Then when I sold her to my friend Jack, he called her Willow, because he thought she should bend (which no doubt meant obey!) How HFF acquired Angel is nothing short of a miracle. Go figure, since God was in charge.

In 2005, when Merrit was in her senior year of high school, she decided to go away to college after graduation. So it was time to find Angel a new home. I had been using her from time to time for lessons, and would love to have bought her. As usual, I had no funds for a purchase so large.

At the time, I had a student named Cadence who absolutely adored Angel, and rode her well. Cadence's parents approached me one day and offered to pay ¾ of her costs if I could pay the other ¼. I was blown away! They insisted that they were only donating the money to HFF and Angel would be totally under my ownership. I'm not even sure Cadence knew about the transaction. What an incredible blessing. What an answered prayer.

As I said, Angel was NO angel—far from it! She was feisty and stubborn and she frustrated many a rider. When you learned how to connect with Angel and push the right buttons, she was a joy to ride. She did have a nasty little problem every month…PMS! Yeah horses can have PMS! During her "time of the month" when she neighed, she sounded like a sick cow.

After paying out $100 a month for hormone shots, my Vet suggested we have her "fixed." So for a mere $2000, we "fixed" 90% of her problem. Best money I ever spent—she was a much better behaved horse—not perfect, but certainly better.

Angel taught many students how to be assertive, and how to listen to her. She won many ribbons with her riders. Cadence had ribbons all the way around her room.

When I decided to retire in 2012, I sold Angel to my friend Jack, who lived in Bishop, CA. Dick and I drove Angel to Jack's, and we talked at length about her and what she'd been doing. I said, "Lessons and trail rides." Jack responded, saying, "She probably needs a little tune up."

A month later he called me and said, "She didn't need a tune up, Marcia. She needed a complete overhaul!" Like

I said, she wasn't a perfect horse, but we sure did love her! Her new name suited her, as Willow learned to bend to her new owner's training.

Jack had Angel for four years. He called me in early September of 2016, to tell me Angel was quite ill. I called Cadence and her mom to let them know. We both decided to jump in our cars (from different cities), and drive to Bishop. It was four hours of driving for both of us.

When we arrived, we spent the day with Jack and Angel. It was a beautiful day—sad, of course, but special because we could be there with her. I Face-timed some of the students that I knew would like to see her and say goodbye. It was a blessing they were able to witness such touching moments in person. Cadence, her mom Robin and I had dinner and then they drove home. I stayed with Jack and his wife Betsy overnight. The next morning, Jack met the Vet at Angel's stable. I just couldn't go…The Vet sedated her and then helped her to cross over the "Rainbow Bridge". She was 19 years old. She was one great horse!

I'm not sure of just which years each horse came to HFF, but they seem to come when I needed them the most. Occasionally, I would have an injured horse and that horse left a "hole" in the lesson schedule. One family in particular was very special to HFF—the Williams—Mike, Sharon, Briton and Amy. They had several horses boarded down the street from me and all had been trained for the Police Mounted Assistance Unit. Nothing scared them. The two we used quite often were Sho-Nee, a chocolate Palamino, and Doc Holiday, a trick horse that Sharon had acquired from Universal Studios. Doc had been trained for the Western Show. If you gave him the right signals, he would bow, rear up, lay down and play dead. Sharon had to retrain him not to lay down and play dead—this was not a good stunt to perform while a student (or anyone, for that matter) was on his back.

Now the signal for him to rear was putting pressure on the middle part of his neck. This was also not a good stunt, especially when a beginner is riding around the arena. I really had to think about who could ride Doc and who shouldn't. Of course, the older more experienced riders loved to make him rear. They soon learned they had to ask me for permission to "rear Doc"—it's amazing that no one was ever seriously hurt.

Both Doc and Sho-Nee were ridden many times in the Rose Parade, either by Sharon or Amy, and sometimes even by a celebrity. I think it was fun for the kids to see the horse they had ridden during a lesson or show on their TV screen in the Rose Parade! Doc and Sho-Nee were wonderful blessings to HFF as were their owners.

Somewhere in the mid 2000's, I borrowed a mare and her three month old foal to have on the farm for the summer. I wanted campers to experience a baby. The little filly came with the name Breezy. The campers had the opportunity to learn how to be around to handle a young untrained horse. By the end of the summer, Breezy was well handled and trained—and I was in love with her. Oh no! What would I do with a young filly? Remember, I was not a horse trainer. I was a teacher.

I bought her for $1000, and my friend who I bought her from allowed me to pay her $100 a month, because, as usual, I had no money. I had always wanted to name a horse and register the name. Breezy was what was called a "Breed Stock Paint". This simply means she comes from registered paint parents, but she had no paint color. However, if she were bred, she could have a horse with a paint color. Her father's name was "Leo's Decka Sonny" and her mom's name was "Cee My Acres". I came up with "Sonny's Breezy Acres" and registered her. For the next few years, my friend Jessica helped me work with Breezy.

I also had a student named Jessica who was instrumental in helping Breezy get a good start. When Breezy was three, student Jessica showed Breezy in her first horse show. I think they won three 3rd place ribbons. Breezy was a great horse and also very calm on the trail. I eventually sold her to a woman who only wanted to trail ride. It was a match made in heaven and "Sonny's Breezy Acres" found a wonderful new home. This horse definitely made her mark on all our hearts and allowed many of us to learn valuable lessons that we would carry with us forever.

I'm still not sure of the timing on all these horses as to when they came and left, but they always showed up when I needed them the most and I know each one of them came from the Lord. God sent them to HFF.

Now "Q"—short for "Qualitynotquanity"—belonged to my equine Vet's husband. Q was a retired Thoroughbred racehorse from the Santa Anita Racetrack. He was a good 16′ hands and a gray. Q had some injuries from the track so he was good for a walk/trot lesson. He had a bit of a habit of dumping his riders, though most didn't mind. They climbed right back on! Q wasn't with us very long but still left a mark on our hearts.

Next there was Rio. Someone told me about a girl who

had outgrown her horse and was looking to sell him. Up to this point, I had spent a lot of time looking at many a horse...ones that would be great for my program or that needed to find a good home. I would usually take several of my students along to "test drive" these horses. I could write books about these "wonderful" horses and their most "interesting" owners.

One horse I went to see was obviously lame. "Oh, he'll be fine by tomorrow," they'd say. Yeah right, I thought to myself! Another horse, even with my best rider, couldn't get him to trot. The owner would then blame the rider. "She doesn't know what she's doing." Again my thoughts were, "Yeah, right!" I thank God He was watching over me. I know I was a "beggar" so to speak. But I also had become a really good "chooser". I knew in my heart that God would be faithful and lead me to the right horse because He always heard my prayers.

A couple of my students and I went to check out Rio, who seemed perfect for the program. Before committing, I requested a short trial period to see how he would do. I think the people were asking $1000 for him. Again, I had no money but I believed God would provide if this was the horse He wanted me to have.

As it turned out, Rio was a perfect fit. The owners insisted on a doing a Vet check before the transaction—which is normally something the buyer would pay for. It was discovered that Rio had cancer in his "private parts." The owners paid for his surgery and I offered to rehab him at my barn since the owners had nowhere to board him. I can't remember how long it took for this sweet horse to heal, but in the end, they GAVE me Rio! Another Godsend. Rio was what we called this Godsend, but his registered name was "Tem bux Two"—not sure where the name Rio came from, but he was an amazing horse and was loved by many. He and ol' Knothead had the same grandfather.

Next up was Pepper and, of course, God's hands were in this transaction too. Rhonda, a friend of mine who worked at Horse Mart where I spent a third of my money every month—a third also went to San Dimas Grain Feed Store and the other third went to Broken Horn Saddlery Store (which many referred to as "Broken Wallet").

Rhonda needed to find a good home for Pepper, so I asked her questions about what Pepper's jobs had been over her lifetime. She was an older horse in her mid 20s. As it turned out, she was a wonderful addition to the farm. She was probably our easiest going horse.

A few months before I was to retire, we were at a horse show in Burbank. We had just finished our classes and were loading up to go home. I had a 4-horse trailer and I loaded Angel in first. Then Jumby. I left a space open and loaded Pepper in the last stall spot. But something spooked Pepper and she went nuts—throwing her body into me which pushed me (and my head) into the wall of the trailer. Not a good situation. Of course, my students and their parents are watching this all unfold! Pepper was tied to the outside of the trailer. I yelled for someone to untie her, and then somehow I was able to drop down on the floor of the trailer and rolled myself into the empty stall. Fortunately, Pepper was in the stall next to the trailer door, and once she was untied, she came out.

I slowly crawled out of the trailer to access the damage of both of us. She was mess with cuts all over her head, but nothing that needed stitches. Thank God. I was dazed with some cuts on my arms and head. But I was more worried about her than me. Someone fetched a bucket of water and we were able to clean up her wounds. In the meantime, people were fussing over me. I felt fine as far as I could tell.

A paramedic who was at the show came over to check on me. By this time I had a bump on my head the size of a baseball—no kidding! It was huge! So with much coercing, I agreed that they could call the paramedics.

Naturally they show up with their lights blazing and sirens blaring—enough to scare all the horses and bringing way too much attention to our corner of the show. I was just a tad bit embarrassed as you can imagine. But it wasn't over yet. Evidently, with a head injury, they suggested that I get it checked out just in case it was serious. So off I went in the ambulance to the hospital. Hmmm, seems like I've done this before. Now with this most unusual way of exiting a show, I was faced with a several challenges.

First I had to call Dick and tell him that I was on my way to the ER... AGAIN! The second was how was I going to get the horses home in my rig? But as you probably have guessed by now, I am not one to give up so easily. Where there's a will (God's), there is always a way.

Erin, my dear friend and most wonderful camp assistant, came to my rescue. Dick brought her to the show arena, and she brought all three horses home and took care of them. I was so relieved. Thankfully, the parents of my students were seasoned show parents, and they stayed with the horses until Erin arrived. I had the best families.

After dropping Erin off, Dick drove over the hospital. By

the time he arrived, our son Scott and his buddy Bert were already with me. I knew Dick wouldn't kill me if the boys were present. Poor guy—I put him through much anguish over the years and he was always a trooper.

I guess God wasn't finished with me yet because everything checked out and I went home with a grateful heart—grateful to God for protecting me physically, and grateful for a somewhat relaxed husband and friends who I could always count on for help.

This incident at the show concerned me. Pepper was pushing 30, and at her last Vet check we realized she was going blind in one eye and almost blind in the other. I think the episode in the trailer made me realize she was having some behavioral problems due to her diminished eyesight. No doubt it scared her not being able to see. She could be a danger to herself and certainly to those people around her.

After consulting with my Vet and her owner, we decided it would be best for her to cross over the "Rainbow Bridge" after I retired, which I was planning to do that March. I watched Pepper very closely that last month. The week after I retired, I took her to a ranch in Monrovia, which my Vet had recommended. The decision was made to donate Pepper's body to the local Vet school (which we also did with Sparkle).

I gave Pepper a tearful hug and thanked her for all she had done for the kids of HFF. Then I walked away knowing that she was in good hands and soon to be free of all pain. I cried all the way home. Some horses are just so special…

Horses would come and go and pass away. It's just what life does. I never got used to it though. Another couple of horses who came to live at HFF were Charlie and Friday. Their owners retained ownership and I leased them. We called it a "feed lease." I simply paid for their feed and housed them. I took care of any Vet bills, but if there were any major decisions to be made regarding the horse, the owner would be the one to make them.

Friday came first. She was a little paint horse who used to barrel race. The kids loved to run on her because she was fast and could turn on a dime! Her registered name was "I'm a Painted Friday". I can't tell you how many campers I asked about what day was the horse named Friday born on? "Saturday" was a typical answer—Really!? Those were mostly answers from the little ones, but occasionally an older student had to think about it! Scary…

Charley came shortly after. He was a flea-bitten Arab. "Flea-bitten" simply means he had a gray body with white hair and flecks of black all over. His appearance looked as though he had been bitten by a bunch a fleas. Charley was a great lesson horse, as was Friday, and both were very popular with the younger riders. When I retired, both horses were returned to their owners. It was always sad to say goodbye, but they were moving on to "greener pastures"...literally!

One of the later horses to join the HFF team was Bentley, whose registered name was "Riding With Style". He was a rescue and a true gift from God! My friend Jess who worked with my Vet called one day and said that my Vet had a horse down at the barn in Portuguese Bend, near the ocean. He seemed to have been abandoned by his owners and had a hoof disease called "white line" infection, and he needed to find a home and be rehabbed. Jess said he was a registered Quarter horse with many "points" for showing under halter. That's where they judge the horse on its confirmation (the horse's form). He was highly trained and was tall for a Quarter horse—16 hands.

I said, "Why not!" Not even sure I ran this one by Dick. Didn't want to hear him say "No!" These people had to have paid $15,000 for him, and I trusted Jess's judgment. I never regretted my decision.

Now Mr. B, as we sometimes called him, came with a few quirks—like bucking. He seemed to do it whenever he felt like he should be finished in the arena—even the show arena! Obviously my more advanced students were the ones to ride him. They either were afraid of him and his antics or found him the challenge that they wanted to conquer.

Before I close out this chapter, there are a few more horses which I need to mention; ones that were graciously lent to me whenever I had a need.

There was Pistol, a lovely chestnut Quarter horse, who belonged to the Nelson family. I taught the Nelson children on Pistol and also on my horse Friday. The last two summers of camp, I needed a fourth horse, and again God provided. The Nelsons were wonderful to lend me Pistol for those last camps before closing HFF, and not surprisingly, she fit right into our routine. Pistol was used for many lessons and activities. But, in my heart, I truly believe her favorite event of all was when the kids would create masterpieces of artwork with finger paints all over her body. Pistol was always so calm and gentle, proving there's nothing like a child's touch.

The next two horses were large ponies; Julie and Grace, who were owned by my friend Rhonda who had given me

Pepper. I borrowed them for lessons near the end of my teachings. They were boarded at a home that was next to Ridge Riders. Several of my helpers would retrieve Julie and Grace when we arrived at the Ridge Riders, and then take them back after lessons were over. My friend Rhonda was so kind to let me borrow them anytime I needed.

And last but not least, there was Mistress, the colorful gray, flea bitten Arab who belonged to Jim, my 80-year-old neighbor. Whenever Jim was visiting at our house, he would love to tell us that he had to go home so he could feed his "Mistress". This would put a smile on our guests and a little confusion as well, until they knew he was referring to his horse.

I never used Mistress for lessons because she was too flighty, but she could run like the wind! Many of my advanced student riders like to ride her when we had a "play day". Play days (or gymkana as we called it) were where everyone played games on horses. My favorite game was "bobbing for apples"... on a horse! The rider and horse were timed. They had to race down to the end of the arena, jump off their horse, bob for an apple (usually helmet and all), and keeping the apple in their mouth, mount the horse and run back to the finish line. Mistress and Angel were my fastest horses so they were the most popular to ride when speed was needed.

Jim's "Mistress" lived way up on the hill next door to us. Whenever I had to go up there to feed, I would take the golf cart and drive up this fairly steep hill on a path that was shaped like a large "S". In order to get to the top, you had to traverse the hill; you couldn't just go straight up.

Sadly, Mistress ended up outliving her owner. After Jim's passing, his wife Audrey stayed on in the house and I continued to feed and care for his horse. I used to wonder what would happen if Mistress died at the top of that hill. It would be nearly impossible to get her down; not like a dog you could carry. She would be 800-900 pounds of dead weight (no pun intended—well, maybe a little.)

Unfortunate for me, Mistress *did* die up there. I went to feed her this one day and she was down on the ground. Not a good sign! I called the Vet and she came out right away. Mistress was still breathing, but she was not in good shape. The Vet and I tried everything to get her to stand, but nothing worked. We needed her up so that we could walk her down the hill. By this time, my friend Jack, who was visiting, came over and Daniel, our right-hand man, showed up. We had plenty of help, but Mistress just didn't have the strength to get up on her own. We knew she was suffering and it wasn't long after that Mistress "trotted over the Rainbow Bridge."

Thankful that Mistress was no longer in pain, but her whereabouts presented a huge problem, not only being up on that hill, but also dying behind the hay barn at the very top. I called the "dead horse guy" and told him our dilemma. He said, "No problem! We've gotten horses off of cliffs and in all other kinds of situations before." I told him to, "Come on over!"

A short time later, the "dead horse guy" pulled up and I took him up on the hill in the golf cart. I noticed him looking around and assessing the conditions. Once at the top, he asked where the horse was and I took him behind the hay barn. I could see his expression as it went from "no problem" to "now what?"

The five of us went over our options—some of which I cannot even write. After much discussion, we decided to pull Mistress down the narrow "S" path with the golf cart. However, we first needed to get her out from behind the barn.

It was Jack who came up with the idea of using a "come along" on the tree that was near the barn. This idea proved successful and we were able to move the horse from behind the barn to the top of the path.

Our next challenge was the sharp bend in the path

halfway down. There was no way we could get the golf cart around the bend and Mistress' body too. Someone would surely fall off the edge, and whoever it was—be it cart or horse—all would be going down. Fortunately, at this bend was where our two properties met and we had a large gate that we could open. Jack drove the golf cart onto our property pulling Mistress behind him.

This grassy area above our arena was secured by a 10-foot block wall. Jack had been able to position Mistress up against the wall and the "dead horse guy" drove his truck up into my arena below. Now came the task of getting the horse up over the edge into the arena and into the truck. She would have to be pushed over the edge. The drop was at least 10 feet.

At this point, I had seen enough. Jack and Daniel were very protective of me and it was at their insistence that I left and went into the house. I grabbed the cash to pay the "dead horse guy" as he would only take cash for his services. The three men used a winch to haul Mistress' body up into the truck. Then the "dead horse guy" drove away with her. I used to wonder about what would happen if Mistress died up on the hill...I wonder no more!

CHAPTER 20

My Boys...

I couldn't possibly write a book without including my two amazing sons. Michael is our first born. He was the first boy in three generations of girls. My father called him the "Golden Boy". Then 6½ years later, Scott came along. We were happy to have a second son, and he was a great addition to our family of four. I had three sisters, so boys' behaviors and habits were all new to me. Many times I'd give Dick a look of "what the heck" when either child was doing something I thought looked odd. Dick would pat me on the back and assure me it was all normal behavior for boys. Like an idiot, I believed him!

By the time I bought my first horse (Knothead), Michael was in college and Scott was in junior high. They thought we were crazy—or least Dad was—to buy the "farm". Remember, we were leaving Dick's dream house. Had I lost my mind? Well, that was to be determined.

I tried teaching both boys how to ride, but they really had no interest, so I didn't push them. I remember one day Michael bringing a girlfriend home, one he had been pretty serious about. I don't know if he thought he was going to impress her by riding a horse, but he asked if they could both come to the arenas where I taught and ride. I naturally said yes. I was thrilled that he was showing some interest.

When the two of them arrived, I put Michael on Knothead and his girlfriend on Rusty. I think I gave them some instructions and off they trotted. Fortunately no one fell off, although I heard there were a few close calls. I learned later that neither of them could walk for days.

Scott went through junior high and high school while my business grew. He discovered the teenage girls that were my helpers and counselors. It was often fun to watch their interactions. The counselors love to tease Scott. I remember one day they toilet papered his room—a large bedroom with a loft. You couldn't see the windows because the toilet paper was so thick. Scott was not a happy camper, to say the least. I think this was a time when he was learning how to graciously "get back all he had given out!"

Scott wasn't old enough to drive and have a summer job. Since the camps were at my house, and so was he, I had to find something for him to do. I decided to put him to work.

I gave him the title of Recreation Director. He was in charge of leading the games on the front lawn.

Scott was a little on the strong-willed side. He wanted to make up his own games and lead them. Not sure how long that lasted, but I was hoping he'd learn to be somewhat responsible. He eventually did become very responsible, but it was years later, and it didn't have anything to do with being my Recreational Director.

Both boys were very supportive as they became older and I could not be more proud of the men they have become. They love and serve God, and are both happily married to strong, amazing women who walk with the Lord.

Michael and his wife Lani have four beautiful daughters: Samantha, Raina, Isabelle and Avery. Scott and his wife Jennifer have an adorable little boy named Harvey. They are all my heart's delight, my pride and my joy!

Dick: Pieces of My Mind, i.e. *My side of the horse empire story (or... life with Joey the hay guy).*

Farm life for me started at age zero in Massachusetts and continued unabated until I was 17. By 1963 I was no longer fascinated by milk, eggs, barn cats, tractors or manure. Way too much manure! So in the nineties when Marcia decided she wanted horses, I was somewhat resistant. And living 20 miles from Los Angeles, we weren't exactly able to homestead on the open range. Just guessing...horse property might be going for more than $50 an acre.

Other considerations were up for review...at least in my mind. Horses weigh over 1000 pounds. They bite, kick and break stuff. Plus they seem to be responsible for enormous quantities of manure. One was so ornery with PMS she had to be "fixed." I recall that was $2500 plus a 600-mile round trip. Hard to imagine New York City in the 19th century with all those tens of thousands of delightful equines tromping around the city 24 hours a day. What did they ever do with all the meadow muffins? Good thing gasoline took over, in my opinion.

I was facilities manager for our ranchette, in charge of infrastructure, such as water, electricity, barn construction, chicken coops and fixing whatever the horses destroyed the day before. One night our ten foot high retaining wall decided to collapse in a rainstorm. A new 80 foot long reinforced 10-foot high block wall cost $40,000 and suggested that we now drove the last new car we would ever own.

Every few months Marcia would suggest an intimate meeting on the front porch around sunset. She would make me a drink. The setting was bucolic. I would begin to fantasize about a romantic liaison. No such luck. But I was guessing that I had better keep a tight grip on my wallet, as the discussion usually drifted toward a new horse, trailer or truck. Those porch chats rarely cost me less than five grand, otherwise known as five "horse dollars." Oh well. Happy wife, happy life.

Our two boys were always hovering around the "sport of kings" but rarely got actively involved. I tried to convince them that horses were "chick magnets." Plus, when daddy took young "Tiffany" to the horse store for expensive riding attire and tack in his $60,000 pickup, I would suggest to our boys that there were lots of worse segments of society to glom on to. The "go-to" local horse store was Broken Horn, which was lovingly referred to as Broken Wallet. Usually full of teens in tight jeans. Enough said.

At regular intervals, I took note of our service providers and their comings and goings. Joey, the hay guy, could be counted on for at least a $250 invoice... plus tip, and when the vet showed up in her $80,000 truck, I knew it would be more than my house payment.

Several other random observations:

Personally, I never had a "truck thing" as an adult.

I learned to drive in a '49 flatbed Ford when I was nine, and by the mid-sixties, I was actually tired of trucks. But Marcia liked them, especially the big ones. The really big ones! During negotiations, the F-250 owner told me "she is really good at pulling stumps." My cupcake had to have it. I preferred the electric golf cart...an excellent manure hauler.

Smaller animals were always part of the mix. One time I left the guinea pigs out in the sun too long and they all died. I was not popular. But, on the other hand, no one ever wanted to be the executioner of the old and the sick, so that became my job. One year Marcia requested that I cut off Glenda the turkey's head. She was half dead anyway (Glenda, not Marcia,) so it seemed the kindest thing to do… unless you happened to be the one with the ax. Even more disturbing, every now and then I would rummage through the freezer only to find a dead frozen rabbit or some species of bird that had recently crossed over the rainbow bridge and someone forgot to tell me. They would all reside in the freezer until trash day.

We also had student sleepovers, mostly girls who I referred to as "the horse munchkins." They giggled all night long. Having only raised boys, this was like a house full of alien life forms. I got used to it eventually.

Finally, one day during the week back in 2005, our God-daughter Tara called me at the office and calmly announced… "They airlifted her to UCLA Medical Center in Torrance." That was the extent of her communication. Turns out Joey, the hay guy left the gate open, and the herd, sensing freedom, instantly galloped down the driveway. Marcia decided to step in front of the stampede, assuming these beasts would just stop in their tracks. Her favorite horse, Knothead, ran right over her. Another day, another crisis.

Amazingly, we never got sued, and Marcia can still walk. Well, sort of...and though I never understood my wife's love of these animals, I did know that what she was doing was important to her and her heart was quite content. And the kids adored her!

Michael: Horse Feather Farm was a part of my life in two different seasons. The first was during my time in college. I occasionally would come home from college during the summer, and witness the anarchy that was the HFF summer camp. House was in shambles; my dad looked like he was on the verge of a mental collapse at the end of every day. Tons of food was always being cooked, primarily by Dale The Iron Chef, or better yet the female equivalent of Gordon Ramsey from Hell's Kitchen. I enjoyed bringing my girlfriend at the time, Jennifer, riding at the Equestrian center. My mom was always very generous with her time, and always took us riding when we wanted to go.

My memory of the leader of HFF, my mother, was one who was respected and admired by both the parents and the children who were fortunate enough to be a part of something this special. In the end, it was chaotic but fulfilling and was a place that changed children's lives for the better.

My second season of life I remembered very well because my two stepdaughters were fortunate enough to attend the camp and take riding lessons. When we would visit, it was a great opportunity for my mom to get to know my future wife as well as her two newly inherited granddaughters.

As time went on, it became the "thing to do" for Sammy and Raina when we would visit, and they always looked forward to learning how to ride and take care of the horses and farm animals. It also gave my wife Lani and me some alone time to go off and have a lunch or dinner date without the kids. It was sort of like daycare, but with horses, goats, saddles, and an incredible Nana as their teacher.

Summer camps were the highlight. They still remember how fun the weekly camps were with all the new friends they made and activities they would do. The summer camps became something we would never miss. One year Lani and I weren't able to drive them down to Southern California, so we flew them on a plane, by themselves and Papa picked them up at the Ontario airport. Lani and I both look back and thought, what in the heck were we thinking? But we could never let the kids miss one of their favorite summer activities!

Horse Feather Farm was a special slice of my life and my family's life that made a Godly impression on us forever. Horse Feather Farm wasn't just a physical place; it was an idea that was built with God as the foundation for students, parents, friends, and family. For everyone that experienced it, I sincerely believe they walked away with wonderful memories filled with love, inspiration, and appreciation for Marcia and Dick Cromie and everyone else who made it possible.

Scott: I write between 700 and 1000 emails a week and, at times, a vain effort to manage anywhere from 6–10 different projects each with very different needs. All of which are ongoing productions across 3 continents, 6 time-zones, with clients that speak one language and developers that speak a multitude of languages, some of which, at times, actually resemble English.

Point being, my life is one that is consumed with language and communication...both spoken and unspoken, written and inferred. Words envelop my life, so much so that powering down the laptop often elicits anxiety, much like putting a newborn to bed for the 5th time, hoping and pleading with God for escape, for rest.

That said, you can imagine the unbridled enthusiasm and zeal I exhibited with every request, reminder, and suggestion—conveniently peppered into every conversation I've had with my mom over the past year—to contribute a chapter to her book.

To the above soliloquy, my mom would say, "It's just like Scott to make this about himself," to which I would reply, "Correct".

Now that I've aired my grievances, let's get to it. Truth be told, I couldn't be more honored to contribute a few choice quips about Horse Feather Farm and the amazing woman at the helm.

My mom's life is one that's marked by giving and

sacrifice; examples she sets both with her words and actions as a mother, a friend, a teacher, and much more to many.

As her son, it's the "much more to many" part that you come to terms with pretty quickly. She was never just "my mom", she was everyone's mom.

The foot traffic at my house was comparable to Costco, with complete strangers often foraging through our kitchen, devouring the "good snacks" and leaving my brother and I to fend for ourselves until around 8:00 PM when mom would either magically assemble a delicious meal from an inconceivable medley of ingredients, OR dad would nearly burn the house down toasting bread (true story).

Either way, we never went to sleep hungry, nor did any of the other temporary occupants in the Horse Feather Farm center for refugees. In addition to the daily pop-ins, we had the regulars who would often, unbeknownst to me, stay the night, turning our family room into a perpetual slumber party.

Now on paper this sounds like a dream come true for any hormone-driven, high school boy – me and a house filled with teenage girls under relatively limited adult supervision. There are countless directions this could go, none of which happened quite the way I imagined.

Instead, the result was often my room being painted with toilet-paper and silly-string like a post-apocalyptic nuclear winter. Before I knew it, I had found myself as the older brother surrogate to a dozen or so younger sisters I'd never wanted; all of whom seemed to derive the greatest sense of joy in the art and mastery of messing with my life.

But once adopted into the Horse Feather Farm collective, they were family. Maybe extended family, like a second cousin once removed kind of thing that you don't really know how they're connected or why they keep coming to family gatherings. But they were family or at least that's how they treated our house and me.

I know the expectation with this is to recount a bunch of stories of what it was like to be a counselor or work for my mom, for that matter. But that's not what I remember. I remember little things.

I remember the wet leather and metal polish laden air filling our family room and kitchen during late night tack prep before a horse show; pizza from Dalias; teenagers with braces; and warm summer nights.

I remember the intensity and hilarity of slaving away next to Dale in the kitchen every morning to prepare lunches for 40 campers and counselors; screaming kids; giant pots of spaghetti, and a fridge that couldn't make ice fast enough.

But most of all I remember the energy of it. It was always in motion. Either we were actively engaged in an activity, lesson, session of the Cha Cha Slide, some amalgamation of the three, OR we were doing the prep work for whatever was next on the agenda.

Horse Feather Farm, wasn't a "tranquil" environment. It was the trading floor on Wall Street. It was chaos ninety percent of the time but mom kept it from coming unhinged like some kind of maestro savant conducting a choir of tone-deaf idiots in her equine opus. It truly was the manifestation of my mom's energy, and she set the tempo for all of us.

She gave her everything to everyone, sometimes at the expense of dad, Mike, and yours truly. But whatever inconvenience or sacrifice we faced as a result of being "Marcia Cromie's support staff" was short term. The lasting effect, both in the lives of those being served and the lives of those being pushed into service were life altering.

In short, while I may not have "appreciated" being asked to give up my room for a family with no home, or my time for kids looking for a place to belong, I couldn't be more humbled to have been a part of something so special to so many people.

CHAPTER 21

The Road to Retirement

It was around 2010 when Dick started thinking about retiring from Southern California Edison. He was 63 and I was 62. He was ready; I wasn't quite there yet. In fact, I thought I'd be this 75-year-old cowgirl with my boots in the stirrups, riding off into the sunset. Yet, I had to admit I was growing mentally weary of my "business." I always enjoyed the physical part...the teaching, the taking care of the horses and their needs. But the financial part was taking its toll. Feed prices were rising steadily and I had growing concerns about having enough money to cover my expenses, especially the feed and Vet bills. Every morning I'd go up the hill to feed my horses wondering if some horse or another animal would be sick or injured with something to warrant calling the Vet. For the more than 20 years that I've had horses, I've been blessed that none had ever really had anything terribly serious happen to them. But that could change at any given time.

As I carried on as usual with the farm and all the animals, Dick started to research places for us to retire, where we could enjoy the outdoors and still afford a comfortable lifestyle. On his search, he came up with Reno, Nevada. Nevada is a great state for seniors— California, not so much. Plus, we both liked the idea that Reno was only three hours from our son Michael and his family in Northern California.

In January 2011, we decided to take a drive up to Reno and look around. Not quite sure why we chose January, but we did! Dick thought he'd make it an adventure and made reservations for us at the oldest hotel in the state, the Gold Hill Hotel, in Gold Hill, Nevada. This quaint little western town is nestled in the hills about 25 miles from Reno.

When we arrived at the infamous hotel, it was 28 degrees with snow on the ground. I loved it! I remember thinking that the hotel really did look like the oldest one in Nevada. But again, we were here for an adventure, right? So we checked in at the registration desk. This desk happened to be in the "newer" section of the hotel. The ladies at our service were very kind and so sweet, but they all looked as if they had been there since it opened!

So off we went to our room, which was also in the "newer" section. Upon entering, we discovered it to be quite warm. After turning down the thermostat, I sat down on the queen size bed ...ugh! It was as hard as a rock. And I was quite certain that the bedspread was an original...kind of a puke gold color. So far, not very impressed.

We were both getting hungry so we freshened up and went down to the dining room. It was decorated like the 1800s—heavy velvet drapes and brass chandeliers. I doubt that the décor was the original one, but they made it to look that way—on purpose. The atmosphere was dark and low key, but we ended up having a lovely time, and our dinner was surprisingly good.

After our meal, we took a tour of the old bar, which was the most original part of the building. The walls were made of rock and wood and were complete with real bullet holes! Interesting, for sure.

When we went back to our room, we found it still very warm, so we decided to shut off the heater and open the windows. But still the room didn't cool down fast enough. We both looked up and saw the big overhead fan above the bed, and Dick was about to turn it on when I yelled, "Stop!" Thankfully, I noticed that on top of each of the five blades there was at least four inches of dust! Had it been turned on, we would have surely experience a very large "dust shower" all over the room.

After another half hour, with the window open and the heat off, we resorted to turning on the small window air conditioning. Dick commented that it would be inefficient (he was my energy expert), but I didn't care. I was hot! Over all, it wasn't the best night, but it was indeed an adventure.

Prior to our trip to Reno, Dick had contacted a realtor. Michelle was a delight and she knew we had no intentions of actually buying a house. We just wanted to see what was available and what the areas were like. Dick and I both agreed that we wanted some property, maybe an acre or more, as I planned to bring Rusty the pony and Rambo the goat with me.

Michelle chose to show us around Sparks, a smaller town adjacent to Reno. Many of the properties had acreage and it was more affordable to live in Sparks than Reno. She took us on a tour of the city and we enjoyed looking around the wide open spaces. Many of the homes she showed us were nice, but nothing really caught our eye. There was no plan to buy. Just look. It was a fact-finding trip only.

Toward the end of the day, Michelle said she had one

more place we might like to see, and it had only been on the market for three days. We drove in the driveway and right away loved the "curb appeal" front yard. Then we opened the door and walked inside. Dick and I looked at each other and we knew immediately that this was the house. What was God thinking? We hadn't even planned to retire for a couple more years! But God's hands were in this every step of the way.

We drove to Michelle's office and wrote up an offer. The rest of it was up to God. If He wanted us to have this house, we knew we would get it. Then we left for the three-hour trip to go visit Michael and his family before we headed back to Southern California.

As we walking up to Michael's front door with our luggage in hand, Dick received a phone call on his cell. I was getting ready to put our suitcases in the spare room when I head Dick say, "We'll take it!"

"Take what?" I asked curiously.

"The house, Marcia! We bought the house in Sparks, Nevada!" Wow, does God work fast or what? I was over the moon excited!

Now the challenge was that we weren't even close to being ready to retire. I know God wanted us to have this house, but I know, too, that it would take us awhile to get everything in order. While we were contemplating our next move, Dick received an email from a woman named Cheryl. The subject title read, "Did you buy the house on Ogden Trail?" Come to find out, Cheryl, our "new" soon-to-be neighbor, was a realtor/property manager. We needed a renter in the house for a year or so, and she found us the perfect family to lease it from us. It was once again our God at work. Our future was beginning to take shape. And we had a wonderful house to look forward to calling our "home in retirement"...whenever that was going to happen!

On our way home from Michael's house, Dick and I discussed a timeline to retirement. All my husband had to do was pick a date and walk out of his office for good. I, on the other hand, had a "farm" to close down. With much thought and many prayers, Dick decided that he would retire at the end of 2012. This plan gave us two years, which was doable.

I know I've said it before, but I'm saying it again. If you want to hear God laugh, tell Him your plan. Then He will show you His. Well our plan was to put our Covina house on the market in March of 2012, and then move to our new Sparks home that summer or early fall. That's not quite how it worked out.

I made arrangements that the last summer camps for Horse Feather Farm would be the summer of 2011. I would continue to teach and "retire" at the end of March 2012. When I sent out the summer camps' brochures, I stated that these camps would be the very last at HFF. To my pleasant surprise, the camps filled up quickly. So many people said how sad they were to see them coming to an end, but no one more than me. Many of the younger siblings of the campers expressed that they too were sad that they wouldn't be able to go because they weren't old enough. I would have loved to continue on with them forever, but I felt I didn't have it in me, and if I couldn't give them my best, I wouldn't continue. It had to be all or nothing.

The summer camps went on as scheduled and ran very smoothly, as did the fall lessons. Now it was time to find homes for many of my beloved animals. This was the hardest part. It was emotionally the most difficult thing I have ever had to do in my life. This was how it all sorted out:

The Bird Aviary: This was basically a large cage (8ft x 4ft x 6ft) made out of wood and chicken wire. It was built by a friend of a friend. Surprisingly (and very thankfully) it even had wheels. When it was given to me, it had a number of parakeets and two cockatiels that came with it. At one point, I added two button quails that eventually killed each other as they fought over who was the biggest and strongest. Neither won! I think we also had a few parakeet eggs that actually hatched and the babies grew into adulthood.

I struggled with how I was supposed to give these birds away. One bird at time seemed too overwhelming to think about, not to mention a very long process. Well, leave it to God to intervene and calm my heart. I had three students who came from one family (a girl and twin boys) and they wanted the cage and all!

Now all we had to do was figure out how to get it to their house which was two towns over. This was when my engineering husband stepped in.

Dick measured the cage and then he measured the horse trailer, and it was a match. The cage would fit in the back perfectly. The challenge would be getting a cage full of birds from the top of the hill to the bottom where the trailer was parked. The new bird owners were on hand to help. Because the cage was on wheels (and they actually worked after all these years), we all gathered around it and rolled it very gently over to the top of the path that went down to the arena. The birds seemed a little concerned at this point, but we moved slowly trying hard not to disrupt their world.

However, as we approached the arena and pushed our way through the deep sand, the birds became a bit unsettled. When we finally reached the steep paved driveway, we had to hang on tight so the cage wouldn't go flying down the hill. As we rolled it ever so slowly down the driveway, our speed began to pick up and the birds freaked out! Feathers were flying everywhere and there were high-pitched screeching sounds coming from inside the cage.

After what seemed like hours, the cage, the birds and all of us finally arrived at the bottom of the driveway, and we continued to roll it until we got it out in the street where the trailer was parked. We stopped so that we could catch our breath and give the birds some peace and calm before attempting to load them.

Fortunately for everyone, the cage was not very heavy, so lifting was not a problem. Once we set it down in the trailer, we realized that Dick's measurement were as close to perfect as they could be, with only about an inch to spare. The group let out a sigh of relief and I thanked God for keeping His critters safe and sound. Now we had to get them home. Once the birds and cage were situated, I got in my truck and drove away slowly, choosing to stay on the surface streets. I thought for sure that a ride on a California freeway would surely do them all in!

We arrived at my students' home with everything and everyone in tact! Then we emptied the trailer of the bird aviary and rolled it gently to its new home under a beautiful shade tree. I said my goodbyes to my little feathered friends and got back in my truck and drove home. With tears sliding down my face, I realized that this was the beginning of the end of this part of my life as I had known it to be for the past 15 years… and my heart hurt. But I continued to trust God. I knew He would find the perfect home for all my beloved animals and feathered friends.

By the time I was ready to retire, Lucy Goosie had passed in her sleep and we, of course, had a ceremonial funeral at our dumpster. Glenda (the turkey) had become so old she could no longer stand. Every morning I would go up the hill and set her up so she was balanced. Then I'd put water and food in front of her and she would gobble (no pun intended) it up. At night when I would go back to check on her, she had fallen over again. So I'd repeat the routine and set her upright and put her food and water in front of her. This went on for a couple months. She seemed happy—me, not so much!

Finally the day after Thanksgiving, I was headed off to teach some lessons, and Dick asked if there was anything he could do for me while I was gone. I said "no" at first. Then I decided that maybe it was time for Glenda to be helped over the Rainbow Bridge. Dick had grown up on a dairy/ chicken farm so I knew that he would know what to do. My youngest son Scott was home as well, and I thought it was time for him to learn a good survival lesson…how to kill dinner!

By the time I returned from the lessons, Glenda had crossed the "bridge" and was buried up on the hill, Dick was reading the paper, and my poor son was looking slightly paler than when I left. I don't think he liked my lesson in survival.

Since this took place during Thanksgiving, you might be wondering why we ended Glenda's life the day after the holiday, instead of the day before. Remember, Glenda was about seven years old. She was a tough old bird, and had we chosen her to be our main entrée at our Thanksgiving feast, we would have had to cook her in the crockpot for at least THREE weeks! Enough said…

There was much work to be done and many animals and

critters to give away. I advertised at the feed stores where I frequented and had also spent a great deal of my money. I had a woman call me from a few towns over who was interested in my ducks and chickens. So I drove out to meet her and to "interview" her. I wanted to make sure she was the right person. She had a few chickens already and had a pretty good setup, so I felt comfortable giving her mine.

She had no way to transport them to her house and offered to pay me to bring them. Dick was with me and knowing his choice, I gladly accepted!

At home we, (yes, Dick and I and Daniel, our forever helper) loaded them all up in cages. We used the manure cart to bring them down the hill. Feathers of all colors were now floating everywhere and the squawking would have awakened the dead! The cages filled my 4-horse trailer to the brim, as we drove ever so slowly to the woman's house.

Now this woman lived in the foothills of LaVerne; up a winding road and a long narrow driveway that went up a steep hill. I don't know how I continued to get myself into these awkward situations, but I seemed to more often than I'd like to remember.

Dick and Daniel looked at the alternatives and there were none. There was no way we could turn in and get up the driveway, and then get back out without bottoming out my truck and trailer. After much discussion, the men decided to hand-carry all the cages up the hill to their new homes. My husband was not a happy camper! It truly is amazing that he has stuck it out all these years!

The next challenge was turning my rig around as this woman's street was a dead end. As I remember, Daniel stood behind the truck and trailer and gave hand signals to Dick who was driving. I thought I could have turned it. After all, I'm the one who drove it all the time. But the men felt they could do it and they were nervous enough—their nerves would have exploded had I been driving!

Somehow they went partially up a driveway that was further down the street and backed down to turn around. All in all it was about a 4-hour ordeal. Needless to say, the money I would have made I ended up giving to Dick and Daniel to split!

The next animals to find homes were George and Gracie, the brother and sister potbellied pigs, and Becky, the black pygmy goat. I received a call from a family in Whittier, CA. They had seen my ad and were interested in the goat. Becky was an easy delivery because she fit perfectly in my red minivan. When I dropped her off, she seemed happy with her new surroundings. A short time later, another family called and wanted to give George and Gracie a home. Ironically, George and Gracie would be living next door to the family who took Becky!

Now transporting these two stubborn very potbellied animals was a different story. The street where these people lived was too narrow to accommodate my truck and trailer. So I chose the red minivan for their delivery too. (A side note: My oldest son Michael bought that van from us when we retired. Maybe he would have thought twice about buying it had he known all the animals that had "graced" the inside seats!)

I called on my good friend Remi (whose daughter Sam was one of my students) to help me. Remi liked animals okay, but she had nowhere near the passion that I did. Bless her heart. She was willing and very gracious. I drove the van into the arena and back behind the barn. Then I backed it up to the dirt driveway and stairs that went up the hill to the pigs' sanctuary.

The scene was similar to the one when we would take George to visit the schools. He was a bit more used to leaving his house, but Gracie was not! She was definitely not a willing participant in this exercise. Armed with long buggy whips and poles, Remi and I tried to "encourage" this pair out of their "house" and into the back of the van. I had fashioned a ramp from one of the wooden stairs to the back of the van—a very thin ramp, according to Remi. She had her doubts that we could get a fat pig over the ramp, and I'll admit it was a challenge.

George came out of his stall fairly easily. Gracie? Not so much. She wanted no part of any of this moving stuff. She cowered in the corner, and was not quiet about her feelings either. You'd of thought we were killing her! My poor neighbors…

I no sooner managed to get Gracie out of the stall and George ran right back in! Remi was beside herself. This was not her cup of tea. At last we got them to the top of the little hill facing down to the van—Remi on one side, and me on the other. Now we did not whip them with buggy whips, although I felt like I wanted to several times. But the whips turned out to be great "encouragement sticks."

We inched our way down the hill—whips in one hand and poles in the other. These pigs were not going back up the hill if I had to block them with my body! Once we got to the base of the hill, we closed in on the squealing pair and were able to shoo George over the thin ramp into the back of the van. Whew—one down, one to go. He snorted his discontent all the way, but he didn't fall off. Success!

Then there was Gracie. She was looking for any loophole she could find to escape this nightmare. I think I saw fear in Remi's eyes, but she was brave and stayed on task. With a little "encouragement" from the whip, she squealed across the ramp (Gracie, not Remi) and nearly ran her brother over! Then I quickly pulled away the ramp, slammed the rear door and off we went to Whittier, which was about a half hour drive. Again, Remi graciously allowed me to volunteer her to help unload these beasts.

There was a whole lot of high pitched squealing in the beginning of the ride, and then it quieted down to a low volume snorting. In fact, I should have given Remi earplugs as she had never heard a pig's squeal before. We arrived safely although I'm sure Remi was questioning our sanity by then.

The father greeted us warmly and showed us where the pigs' new home would be. I felt that they would be very happy in their surroundings as well. But first, we had to get them out of the van and into the backyard.

I had forgotten my makeshift ramp so the two of us (poor Remi) had to lift them out of the back of the van and onto the driveway. George was the lightest of the two at about 80 pounds. Gracie, on the other hand, was a "foodie" and weighed close to 100 pounds. I could see Remi rolling her eyes and thinking "What have I gotten myself into, lifting fat, squealing pigs out of a minivan? This is one for the book!" In the end, Remi and I were successful of ridding my vehicle of the little porkers. Fortunately for us, I had remembered the "encouragement sticks" and we were able to guide them back to their new abode.

I thanked the family profusely and we left. I don't remember Remi saying much of the return trip home. I think she was mentally and physically exhausted. I certainly was. What's amazing is that she is still my friend today.

The horses I still had in my care at the time I was going to retire were: Jumby, Bentley, Rusty, Angel, Friday, Charley and Pepper. These animals were the toughest to part with. I loved them all so dearly. After my last lessons at the end of March 2012, I dispersed all the horses except Rusty. I had decided that I would take Rusty and Rambo the goat with us since we had over an acre at our new home in Sparks. The plan was that we would build housing for them before we moved. Again, if you want to hear God laugh, tell Him your plans! More about what happened later…

Friday and Charley were on loan to me and were tearfully returned to their owners. Friday went back to her owner's barn to be fully retired. Charley was retired to a pasture north of L.A.

In September of that same year, I received a phone call from Marisa who I had given Kali to. Kali was down and the Vet was on her way. I rushed over to Marisa's house and waited for the Vet. Kali was 30 years old and had been having some problems. I knew it was time to say goodbye. When the Vet arrived, she confirmed my thoughts. We said our tearful goodbyes as Kali peacefully crossed over the "Rainbow Bridge."

Kali had been one of my favorites—my beautiful gray (white) Arabian. She really was stunning. She had been a great lesson horse to all my HFF kids. Marisa and I had a good cry afterward and said our own goodbyes with promises to keep in touch.

On the way home, I received a phone call from my friend Jess who worked for my Vet. She had just found out that Charley had passed away in the pasture where he had been taken to live out the rest of his life. And he did. How ironic—my two beautiful Arabs crossing the "Bridge" together! Pepper, sweet Pepper, as I said before, had crossed the "Rainbow Bridge" right after I retired, and while living in Bishop, CA with my dear friend Jack, Angel had passed in September 2012.

Now I had my beautiful Jumby Bay and Bentley to find homes for. They were both 12 years old and in great shape. I would have loved to have taken them to Nevada, but I also wanted to stay married!

Over the years that I had Jumby, I had much of her training done with the help other another trainer named Karen. I liked Karen's training method and thought that many of my students would benefit from her skills when I retired. I approached Karen one day to see if maybe she would have an interest in Jumby and Bentley joining her barn. Turns out she did, so I sold each of them to her for one dollar. We made up a contract, which gave me first "rights" to buy them back if I ever wanted. This gave me peace.

The day after I retired, I brought them to her barn. At that time, she had an open "house/barn" to welcome my students. Many of them came to meet Karen and joined her barn. Nowadays, I visit Jumby and Bentley when I am down in "SoCal". I have even offered to take them both when they're ready to retire. I don't think Dick has read this memo so Shhhh. Let's keep this between us!

Well last but not least...Rusty. Remember I had planned to take him and Rambo the goat to Nevada. Our plans were to sell the house and move to our new home by the summer of 2012. Well, I can still hear God laughing. The house was on the market for six months... without one offer!

As we anxiously waited for the house to sell through the spring and summer months, I saw Rusty's health decline, and started to have some serious reservations about taking him to cold weather country.

In early August, I was getting ready to take Angel to Jack's place in Bishop. The Tuesday before I was to leave, I decided to take Angel and Rusty to Ridge Riders one last time. Cadence and Allegra wanted to ride Angel one more time. When we got there, Rusty hung out in the trail arena and soaked up the warm summer sun, and the girls took Angel for her last ride in the Ridge Rider arena.

Upon returning home, I led the two horses up to their stalls. But it was obvious that Rusty was not quite right. Later, I went up to feed, and Rusty was laying on the ground—not typical. His breathing was off so I called the Vet. We discussed the possible outcomes. I knew in my heart it was time, but I wasn't ready. Not sure I would ever be. My dearest of ponies, who had given so much, to so many...I wanted him to live forever!

After struggling to get him up, I walked him down to the arena behind the barn. He immediately laid down again. My heart was breaking. I had opened the gate so the Vet could drive up to the arena when she arrived. All of a sudden, Rusty jumps up and proceeds to race around the barn a couple times and then bolted through the gate and down the driveway!

Oh great, I thought. Sylvia the Vet will be driving up the street any minute and see the pony running past her…the same pony she's supposed to be putting down! Fortunately for me, my sweet neighbor Carlos, who was also a horse owner, was able to stop Rusty and bring him back.

I was already in the street when Carlos came around the corner with my horse. I led Rusty back up the hill to the arena where he promptly laid down again. Within moments, the Vet arrived. She took his vitals and I could see in her face the prognosis was not good.

By now Dick was with us, holding me up. As I write these words, tears are streaming down my face. If ever there was a special pony, it was Rusty. Saying goodbye to this one would be the hardest thing I have ever done. As Sylvia prepared to send him over the "Rainbow Bridge," I knelt down and hugged his head and neck, and thanked him for all he given us. Sylvia had given me some scissors and I clipped some of his thick, black mane to remember him better. When Rusty took his final breath, I fell into the arms of my loving husband, sobbing my heart out. Dick had always been there for me, and I am forever grateful.

After the Vet left, Dick insisted that I go inside and that he would wait for the "dead horse guy" to come. God knew that I would need a man like Dick who was my rock and support from the very beginning. I think all those days growing up on a dairy farm taught Dick a lot about life and death with farm animals and he understood better than most.

Four days later, I hauled Angel up to Bishop. When I got home and looked over the landscape, I saw a much different setting—the barn, the pipe corrals and the cages were all empty for the first time in 12 years.

The days dragged on and still there were no offers on the house. I would often walk up to the top of the hill and sit under the century old oak tree and cry. I missed every animal and bird that graced these barns, corrals and cages. They were my friends. We had traveled through so much together, each of them with individual personalities, even the birds. I learned to care for all of them, and they, in turn, taught me patience and love.

I would sit there and think about the greatest gift God

could have ever given me. And what He gave me was "the desires of my heart." Not just one horse, mind you. He gave me many! And because He gave me many, I could give to those young girls and boys the desires of their hearts—to know and to love a horse.

I often thought to title this book, How God Created and Sustained HFF. It was His gift, not only to me, but to all who experienced "the farm". I really wrote this book for my students and their families. I wanted them to know how HFF was created. It wasn't me. It was all from God. It was part of His glorious plan. I'm just so very grateful He chose me to carry out this part of the plan.

So for now I say, "Goodbye, and may the Lord bless all my students and their families and all who have read this book. It is my prayer that you will find God's plan for your life, too, and that He gives you the desires of your heart."

"For I know the plans I have for you," says the Lord, "plans to prosper you and not to harm you, plans to give you a hope and a future" (Jeremiah 29:11).

"May he give you the desire of your heart and make all your plans succeed" (Psalm 20:4).

Memories

Staff, Campers & Parents...

Horsey days gone by

Mikayla: Wow, I have so many great memories from camp, it's hard to pick just one! I loved horse camp so much and looked forward to going every summer. Among my favorite memories were picking blackberries in the creek, playing games in the front yard with all the kids and, of course, grooming and riding the horses!

Horse/farm camp instilled in me a love for animals and interacting with them. I am now finishing up high school and volunteering at an equine therapy center! We do physical and mental therapy for kids with CP, autism, and other conditions. We also do rehabilitative care for people who have been in accidents or have been through trauma. I would not have been able to lead riding lessons nor properly care for the horses and the safety of the children if I had not gone to horse camp with you. Thank you for everything, Marcia!

Jan: Max remembers eating lunch under the tree and competing with Josh for good manner stickers (holding open the door etc.). I remember Max flying off a horse. Kendall remembers washing the horses, and one kicked a bucket of water into the garage, how the horses loved to roll in the dirt after the saddles came off. Courtney remembers painting the horses and how much fun that was. I think they were actually surprised that you let them do that. He also remembers riding in the van with all the tack to go to the other arena. Tori remembers the hard work involved in brushing the horses. She learned unique skills and doing crafts, getting a 'most helpful' award. Her favorite horse (probably for all of them) was Sparkle. I think Josh might have been a bit fearful of the large animals, but he was able to overcome that and go into a trailer to bring one out. He and Max had a great time together living the "cowboy" life.

Lauren: My memories of Horse Feather Farm are amazing to look back on. I remember the care-free times we spent playing riding games, going trail-riding, having water fights on hot days, visiting different houses with swimming pools, blackberry picking by the creek, tie-dying t-shirts, painting the horses, and participating in many more fun activities. Looking back, however, I can most clearly remember days that were on the more difficult side. When I was a young camper, I did not understand why learning how to muck stalls or clean tack was so important. It definitely was not fun, but it was a responsibility that we had to take care of. HHF was the first place where I had responsibilities that were not going to be taken care of by anyone else.

As a young adult, the memory of this unfavorable chore instilled in me a sense of responsibility, as well as a broader understanding of why I should accept the task given, and do it to the best of my abilities. Learning how to take care of different animals can be fun, but it is also hard work. When I tell people of my experiences at HFF and how a city girl like me used to run around a farm all day feeding chickens, cleaning stalls, giving goats baths, etc... they are always pretty surprised.

Working on a farm is something that not many people experience, although it is truly a place that teaches many lessons. Learning how to take care of living things teaches us not only responsibility but empathy. Having empathy for animals and learning to understand them is a skill that can be translated into any part of life where we interact with other people. Empathy for animals teaches us to have empathy for other people, to be willing to see where they are coming from, and why they are acting a certain way. I like to think that the empathy I learned from HFF is what led me to be interested in psychology, the study of the human mind and behavior, and sociology, the study of society as a whole and the influence of society on the individual.

Indeed, empathy is something that is badly needed in the world today, and I am glad I learned it early on in such a great way. HHF was a place where I learned some of the most important life lessons anyone could learn. And Marcia, I would like to say that you were absolutely integral to my success as an adult today.

Nancy: Your program gave Lauren her riding start and also the opportunity for my dad to see her ride in a horse show before he passed away (horse shows were a HUGE part of my childhood). Seeing Lauren on a horse was a great gift to him. Your program also got me back in the saddle after an eight-year hiatus. Say what you want about Bentley, but I loved that horse! The best part of HFF is that it was a friendly and supportive program. I think fondly of our time with you.

Rebecca: As you know, I had started riding with Karen about four years ago. Sadly, I was only able to ride with her for two years though. I did end up showing Bentley in Long Stirrup and Green Rider. Our most successful classes were typically the Hunter Under Saddle classes and the Hunter Derby classes.

Currently, I am on the IHSA Western Show Team at Cal Poly San Luis Obispo. I still try to ride English as much as I can because I feel it is essential to get familiar with and be competent with as many styles of riding as possible. They all have their strengths and similarities. Last year, our Western team qualified for Semi-Finals for the first time in many many years which was very exciting.

Thank you for starting me off the right way and showing me that it is not just about taking lessons and riding that makes you a horse person. Nevertheless, looking back I think the horse that taught me the most was Angel because she challenged me. She made me realize not every horse is just going to do whatever you ask of them. She was humbling.

I don't have many specific memories since I was pretty

young especially to start. However, I do remember always being excited to go to Ridge Riders even if it was just to watch my sister in a lesson. I think the two things I remember most were the horsey birthday parties and handing out ribbons at some of the shows. I remember I was so proud of myself when you let me ride by myself at one of the parties, and I got to show all my friends how cool it was that I could ride without someone leading me. Even though I always wished that I could be the one showing, I am glad I waited until I was older. It was again a good humbling experience, and it taught me that volunteering could be rewarding and fun.

Horse Feather Farm provided me with a solid, well-rounded basis that has made everything I have achieved so far possible.

Victoria: The way I met Marcia is probably one of the most embarrassing moments I've had. I was young, about 14 when I googled 'Horse Back Riding Lessons'. Now, she wasn't the first result that came up as at the time she was part of the Cameron Park Community Center, so when I found them, I asked for a ride from my parents to find out more. I was given a flier with some information about Ridge Riders Equestrian Center, though it was hard to believe it existed at all considering it was right in the middle of the city, tucked away behind a baseball field. It was practically invisible. On that flier, was Marcia's information, including her email address. It took a lot of courage, but with as much professionalism as I thought I had, I wrote my very first message to her. I remember I asked her how much lessons cost and how long they were. She kindly answered all my first basic questions.

What no one knew at the time was my parents were going through a very rough divorce. I was the oldest of four and still only 14, so I felt like so much of the world was on my shoulders and I needed an outlet. I had a passion for horses as long as I could remember, so much so that friends at school made fun of me for it. I had horse folders, spiral notebooks, stickers, even books on how to care for horses, though I didn't have any myself. I still have the collection.

With the divorce ongoing, I tried not to bother my parents too often, so I knew that when I approached them with this proposal, I needed to have all the facts and details. That was where my emails to Marcia became more frequent. I even remember a three-email conversation about what boots I should bring. It was something we bonded over for a long time.

After my first lesson, I was hooked. I was introduced to Rio, who immediately became my favorite horse. I felt comfortable around him, and for a beginner, he was wonderful. He gave me confidence, and I looked forward to seeing him and Marcia every Wednesday for my hour, but with a passion for horses like mine, that hour quickly started not to be enough. I wanted to spend more time there, so I stayed after my lessons, and watched all the other girls' who had lessons after mine. When something needed to be done, I would always volunteer. Any time I could get my hands involved in helping out, I was always the first one to jump. It meant I got to stay a little longer and spend more time with the horses. Though, with staying longer, it also helped me make all my new friends. I had the pleasure of meeting Halee, Jessica, Lorrinda, Julianna, Heather, Anna, Sarah, Hannah, Cadence, Allegra, and Victoria.

I never told anyone this, but there came a point in life where my family was struggling. With the divorce, I ended up moving in with my grandmother and my mother, so there ended up being five people in one bedroom. Money was extremely tight, but I needed to keep my happy place. It was the first time I ever opened up to Marcia. I remember trying to catch her alone and sitting down on a bench late at night. I told her that I wanted to continue, but my family was struggling. I had been around to help often, so she made me a proposition. She told me that if I not only continued to help out as I had been with all the lessons and getting horses ready for their riders, but I went home with her as well to help feed and care for the horses after, that it would make up for my hour lesson. I was so grateful to her for that. I never forgot it, and it only pushed me to work that much harder. But I was also excited because it opened up another door for me. I got to see the magic that happened "behind the scenes"...more time with the horses and more time with all the girls that had become my friends. This work I did was not work to me.

I was so happy. I now came as often as I could. Three to four days a week, from early morning until about four or five at night. Sometimes we stayed even later than that as lessons sometimes ran a tiny bit behind. I also helped out at all the shows. I didn't usually ride in shows. I never thought I was quite ready, but I would be there to support my friends and my team.

After Marcia's proposition, things changed for me. I was so much happier. As long as I worked hard and did my best, I had a place. I had a home. I learned to love country music, which to this day I still love. Marcia instilled in us not to swear. She didn't care if we swore like sailors at home, but not when we were together at the farm or during lessons. She taught us how to run a business without having to do it verbally. We all learned by watching. She went above and beyond just being a horseback riding coach. She was our caretaker while we were with her.

If anyone was hungry during lunch time without money to pay, she always (without hesitation) paid for them. Some of my best memories are lunchtimes. We always had a buddy system to go down to our favorite place on the corner; Classic Burger. Their onions rings and teriyaki bowls were all of our favorites. They also had delicious grilled cheese, and of course, we could never forget the extra ranch dressing everyone loved. We all grew up together.

I was a huge fan of The Saddle Club. I never in my life thought I would find something like it, and in all honesty, I found something so much better. I met Anna and Sarah because I taught them the basics. What I learned from Marcia in my lessons, I applied to their lessons. They were maybe seven or eight-year-old twins when I started to teach them. Now I see them on Facebook, and I can't believe the young ladies they are. I see them continuing their lessons, owning their own horses now, and I can't help but feel so proud to have been a part of their life. Marcia gave us all a bond we can't break. All these years later, and we all still check up on each other. We all care, and we're all that tight-knit family.

Marcia also taught us how to cook! I remember when we had camp or a show to get ready for, we all spent the night at her house. She taught us how to make eggs in a basket, blackberry pie with ice cream, and fruit salad with cinnamon. She even introduced me to quiche! I had never had it in my life. But then at a party at her house, she encouraged me to try it, and I did! It was so good! She used to tease all of us and tell us the morning of a show that if the chickens didn't have any eggs, we didn't eat. At Horse Feather Farm, we also learned how to be prepared for the unexpected. With animals sometimes unpredictable, we needed to plan ahead and think about things before they happened. We had to know what the consequences of our choices were because it had everything to do with safety. We had to think of people before ourselves. It's something that I still do to this day. She also taught us, with the help of her animals, to learn how to forgive. Whether it was a friend or the horse you were riding, forgive them and move forward. So you fell off because the horse spooked? Forgive them because they didn't mean it, and come and join the ice cream sundae club. It kept our confidence and, more importantly, helped us stay as close as we were. If we could forgive people the way we did our animals, there was nothing we couldn't do, and we could all grow and learn from the experience. It still rings true.

Marcia also taught us how to love and how to lose. When I first started riding, I met Rio. I didn't know he was an older horse, and so his time to leave us happened about three years into knowing Marcia. I took the news of his death so very hard. I never expected it to hurt as if he had been my own, but it did. I didn't come back to Horse Feather Farm for three months. I don't know how Marcia knew, but she did, and she called me. She told me that not riding wasn't something he would have wanted and that I would be honoring him and everything he had taught me by coming back and moving forward. She told me she understood it was difficult, but that things weren't the same without me, and more importantly there were others than just myself that missed him who needed someone to lean on. I hadn't thought about it that way, and once again, I rejoined my family and kept going. I had to be strong for them just like I had to learn to be strong at home with everything that was going on.

Marcia and her husband Dick came to me when I needed them most. They were there for all the events a teenager would have considered monumental. My first break up, I was consoled by Marcia; when things got rough at home, she was always the one to offer her loft for me to sleep in. I learned to drive and got my license while doing things at Horse Feather Farm. You didn't even need a reason to see her; all you had to do was call and ask if you could come over and she never refused you if she wasn't busy.

Her dogs, Buddy and Freckles, and her cat Toby, they were your dogs and your cat too. She made you part of her family. There's a picture of me sitting on a set of bleachers at a show I'll never forget. I had been helping all morning and had a chance to sit down, and she took it so I would know I was just as important as the girls in the arena. She was and still is family to me...she made me into the person I am today, and I have no idea where I would be as a person without her teachings of forgiveness, patience, and kindness.

I remember talking to Anna and Sara about the movies and how uncomfortable it had to be to ride two people on one horse. Somehow, we thought it would be interesting to find out, and while trying to lift one of the twins by the hand with my own up onto the horse, we both fell off. She ended up pulling me down, and we landed on top of each other. We laughed so hard laying on the ground we were crying.

I also remember feeding the horses at night sometimes, and we were in the shed preparing meals when the handle would jiggle like someone trying to come in. Lorrinda and I were inside and screamed suddenly when the door flew open only to find that Rambo the goat had learned to open the door using his horn just to be able to help himself to some food. Needless to say, a lock ended up going up on the inside so that we would lock the door behind us, but it didn't keep him from trying.

I remember going to pick blackberries from the creek near her house for summer camp with all the campers. I stepped into the creek not knowing that there were crayfish in the water walking over our feet. I had never felt anything like it, so when one decided to crawl over my foot, I jumped and ended up sitting in water waist deep.

One of my favorite things was when Marcia would call me asking if I wanted to help with a birthday party or to do a charity event. I always loved seeing the kids faces light up when we brought the horses or even the pigs sometimes.

Another one of my fondest memories was my first play day. I remember it was Halloween and I spent weeks working on a blanket for Rio to make him look like a knight's horse, and I dressed as a princess. We won first place, and I was so proud.

I also remember spending the night at Marcia's house before a show. Four or five of us would sleep up in the loft, and instead of sleeping, we would spend most of the night wide awake. Then about an hour before we needed to be up, we would fall asleep. When it was time to be awake, we were all zombies walking up to the back of the house and up to the horses. We would regret not falling asleep sooner, but the next time there was a show, we were all at it again.

These are only a handful of all the great memories I have. I have so many that I can't count all of them. While I am here writing my memories though, I want to thank you, Marcia. You were there for me when no one else was. You were there to be the mother figure I needed in what I felt to be a part of my life where I felt like I was drowning. You opened up your life, and your home to me and I am forever grateful for it. There isn't a day that goes by that I don't think about you, and I apply everything you taught me to my everyday life.

I'm now living in Denmark, and I'm married to a great guy. I'm also in the process of opening my own cosmetics line while also trying to finish school. I'm doing a lot at once, but I'm happy. I keep in touch with all the girls still. We all check up on each other, and I constantly check up on all of them.

Brittany: There are too many things to remember, from my first day as a camper to the last day as a counselor. But if I had to choose one, I would choose the one week of Winner's Circle that I went to. There you taught me how important trust is and what it was like to be a camper all over again. All the other memories will be cherished forever. I will definitely miss you!

Sara: I have so many memories at HFF. Marcia was like a second mother to me and I know that she will always be there for me, like she was when she was teaching me lessons to ride. It was so much fun. I love you so much and you will always be so dear to my heart.

Jezi: I liked the horses that you had. You made me not afraid of them anymore.

Danielle: Thank you so much for helping Jezi with her self confidence and her confidence around animals. I will be forever grateful. Jezi's mom.

Tati: Write down a few fun memories of Horse Feather Farm? Where do I even start? There have been so many wonderful memories that I could probably write my own book. I guess I'll start with September 2000. I wish I knew the exact date, but I do remember it was the first week of 7th grade at Sonrise Christian School. My mom and I had recently moved from Huntington Beach to West Covina to be closer to my grandma. My riding initially started at Huntington Central Park. I was devastated when we moved because I didn't know that I would be able to ride again, but after being enrolled at Sonrise, my mom found out they were starting up a new equestrian program. There were no words to describe my excitement; to this day, I still remember that feeling.

I wasted no time talking my mom into letting me start lessons again with Marcia. That first weekend of school was my first lesson. I'll never forget it; we had just walked into the house and Scott, her son, had stormed in and slammed his books on the ground and went off to his room. Clearly, he had had a rough day at school. Marcia turned around and said, "Welcome to Horse Feather Farm!" We laughed and wandered out the back, up the ramp, and into the barn area. My first lesson was on Knothead. Marcia asked if I had cantered yet back in Huntington. I said no, and she said, "Well today is the day," and with one simple cue, I finally got to canter. To this day, I believe Knothead had the bounciest trot, but his canter was smooth as can be.

It wasn't long before I started my lessons up at Ridge Riders. At first, my mom would drop me off at Ridge Riders for my lessons, and we would leave right after, but I usually would beg to stay longer. Next, I'd beg to stay and help bring the horses home. Soon after that, I'd ask to be dropped off at HFF to help load, and I'd stay all night or day until we loaded up to go back to HFF. Rambo the goat, who thought he was a dog, would always be with us. I remember him even sitting on Marcia's lap while she drove down to Ridge Riders. All of us would have our fun with him, and then he would wander off to terrorize horses nearby.

Marcia would always refer to her trailer as a four and

a half slant trailer. Which brings me to one of my favorite horses, or should I say pony. Rusty was the "half" slot of the trailer. I'll never forget the first day I got to ride him. There weren't many who got to ride this pony. At the time, it was mainly Katie and me sharing him. If there was anything that crazy pony taught me, it was Marcia's favorite line, "Patience is a virtue." And patience is exactly what you needed. A whole lot of patience, but Rusty made every single ride count, especially at the shows. My favorite part about showing Rusty had to be the jumpers' classes. That little pony could jump the moon and turn on a dime until he decided that he was done for the day. Then he'd start darting to the right or left right before the last line or very last jump, and there was no way you were going to make him finish that course.

Looking back, I think it was Rusty who taught me the most about being a rider. To always think ten steps ahead of your horse, learn how to read them, watch their ears, learn to be patient, understand that they are much bigger than you and have a mind of their own, and definitely learn how to sit and hold on. Rusty may have been small, but I don't think any other horse has ever taught me so much.

Then one day my world came crashing down, or at least I

thought it did. Little did I know it was one of the best things to happen to me. After being grounded from riding lessons, which I'm sure had something to do with my grades, I was finally back to ride and ran straight for Rusty and hugged him. I was so excited to ride him again. Then Marcia broke the news and said I had outgrown him, and it was time to move onto a bigger horse. I can't remember if I showed how upset I was or not, but I literally thought my world had ended. That's when I was introduced to the Arabian breed.

Kalendar Girl was a gorgeous gray purebred Arabian. There was no denying I thought the mare was pretty, but she wasn't Rusty. However, it didn't take long for me to bond with Kali. Especially after our first show. Kali won me my first blue ribbon that day, and after that, there was no stopping us. From shows at Ridge Riders to shows in Chino, Kali always knew when it was time to show and she never disappointed. Little did I know, Kali had a much bigger impact on me than I thought she would have. Knowing now what I know about Arabians, she was everything you'd ever want. Kali never batted an eye, did everything you asked (except jump, that was not going to happen), toted many beginner kids around the arena, took care of her riders in the show ring, and brought home many blue ribbons for her kids.

Sadly, in July 2003 my family and I moved to Las Vegas. Looking back, I still remember how heartbreaking that was for me. I wasn't worried about having to move to a new city and making new friends. I was devastated that I was leaving Marcia and the entire HFF family. My mom promised I would finally get to own a horse in Vegas and let me tell you, I didn't waste any time looking for one. Within a month I had found Sophie, a Quarter Horse. A short time later, I found my second horse, BB Bonnie Blu, aka Bonnie, a fiery 18-year-old Arabian.

Marcia and HFF taught me so much. HFF was really the foundation of the rider I have become today. Whenever I'm having a rough ride, I always hear Marcia saying, "patience is a virtue." One of the biggest things I learned was that it wasn't all about winning a class, it was about going out there and doing the best you can and, most importantly, having fun. HFF was my second home for three years. My time there had such a great impact on my life. These memories I will cherish forever. The friendships I've gained are ones I could never get anywhere else. All the horses of HFF hold a special place in my heart. Every one of them played an important roll in my first few years as a rider, and for that, I am forever grateful. I couldn't be more thankful for Marcia and all the life lessons she has taught me, even if I didn't realize back then what the lessons meant. This is one friendship I am truly blessed to have; it's been 17 years, and I wouldn't trade a second of it.

Thank you, Marcia, for all that you have done, not just for me, but for every kid that has been a part of HFF. I hope you realize how much you have impacted all of us, especially me.

Sharon: This is a true story of young ladies who choose blue jeans, boots, dirt, and horses over short shorts, tight fitting tops, and boys. Their perfume is od de horse (or duck, goat, chicken) and instead of make-up, streaks of sweat, dirt, and horsehair. And they couldn't be a happier bunch.

This incredible group of young ladies was brought together by my friend Marcia Cromie, at a time of changes and turmoil, and not just because little girls are transitioning into young women. The LA Riots are still fresh in our minds, an economic downturn affects many families, our community is turning open spaces into mini-malls and condominiums, and then our country is attacked and forced into war with the Middle East. Our youth are facing adult decisions before they have the ability to deal with adult consequences of those adult decisions. It's Marcia's idea for Horse Feather Farm that inspires hope and teaches responsibility, builds confidence, and instills the importance of character with integrity to these soon to be women.

Looking back at Horse Feather Farm, I have come to realize Marcia was the mentor. The real teachers of life lessons were the horses, like the sweet mare Angel who turned into a cranky, inconsolable beast during her heat. Who couldn't relate?

There was Rambo the goat, who had his own mind and was often the renegade who loved eating everyone's food when they weren't looking, and the sport of being chased by the girls when everyone wanted to go home. The ducks, geese, and chickens made eggs and babies. And everyone got along because it was a happy place, and wonderful, sweet, smelly refuge.

Not all children are suited for team sports such as baseball/softball, soccer, etc. Marcia's Horse Feather Farm filled the void for young girls and boys who for whatever reasons found themselves not fitting in with their school peers. With Marcia's program and animal teachers, the shy participants became active leaders; the unconfident became fierce competitors in the horseshow ring; the unfocused became taskmasters; the impatient learned patience.

Having recently gotten word our beloved community equestrian center is in danger of closing as so many others have already in Los Angeles County, I have had the opportunity to reconnect with the Horse Feather Farm "girls". They are all now successful, working women. The comments I have heard from them are all similar in nature. The years with Marcia's Horse Feather Farm and Ridge Riders Equestrian Center were the best of their lives. They credit Marcia and the animals for "saving my life" and giving them the real-life skills they needed to be successful, confident, and happy adults. As for me, it helped me feel young again, and optimistic about the future knowing these young women would be entering the adult world with confidence and a loving, caring and compassionate spirit.

UPDATES: Amy is currently working for the Los Angeles County Sheriff's Department as a Sheriffs Security Officer. She is the first SSO to be integrated into the Sheriff's Department Mounted Enforcement Detail. She is one of only forty members of this 7000 strong law enforcement agency to be on the mounted enforcement detail. She is using Dudley as her police horse. I am now retired after 36 years in law enforcement. Doc and ShoNee have joined most of the HFF horses in God's eternal pasture. My favorite times were meeting with you and girls after work at Ridge Riders and our dinners there, after lessons. And, of course, the Halloween play days!!

Lorrinda: I was introduced to Marcia and Horse Feather Farm when I was around six-years-old when I nonchalantly walked into Ridge Riders Equestrian Park (which is attached to Maverick Baseball field), not knowing the heart attack I was going to give my mom in the process. The very moment I saw those horses tied to the trailer, I was hooked. But it wasn't just the horses that got me hooked to Horse Feather Farm. The people that I met made me love it even more. Growing up with Marcia she quickly became my second mother. She taught me a lot of life lessons that I still use to this day. But the lesson I remember most is when you fall off the horse, you have to get right back on. And after a bad fall off Marcia's horse Knothead, which resulted in me breaking my wrist, that is a lesson I quickly learned. When it came to Horse Feather Farm you weren't just with friends; you were with family, cause to me that's what Horse Feather Farm was, my horse-crazy family.

Isabelle: I still look back fondly on my time with you, even though it was only a couple of years. You gave me a place to ride with lots of other kids my age, and coming from Bonelli Park, where Pam Cozad and her daughter Alicia had been giving me lessons, that was huge. Bonelli had mostly adults, and I never saw other kids regularly enough to make friends. It was a big deal for me to meet other horsey kids through you!

My second summer with you, I was a CIT at camp all summer. You and Sara and Anna taught me how to teach kids to ride. After you moved, I helped teach special needs kids to ride for awhile and used a lot of the tricks I'd learned with you. For example, telling kids to pretend they were reaching for cookies on their mount's butt when turning!

All the time I spent with you in lessons on Jumby, taught me never to give up, and that if I believed I could jump, she would jump. I learned a lot about perseverance and willpower from Jumby!

Now I'm in my third year of college at UC Santa Cruz. This summer I was a camp counselor at Galileo summer camp in Los Feliz, for their Kindergarten age group. As counselors, we tie-dyed shirts one evening, and I could still remember how to make hearts and peace signs and lots of other designs from that last summer with you. Lots of the camp songs and games I played with my kids were things I learned at camp with you.

I still love horses, although I haven't ridden much in recent years. I'm majoring in Environmental Studies and Biology, and I'm going to study abroad in Bordeaux, France this spring. I'm still trying to figure out how to make horses a part of a future job! Thank you for all you did for me, Marcia, and everyone else at Horse Feather Farm!

Galen: I can't help but smile when I reminisce about the countless riding lessons I had or the fun of summer camp. This past summer during my field training, I was pulling security in a patrol base in the middle of the night, in the rain. I am not going to lie, I was pretty miserable! I was soaked through my waterproof jacket, poncho, and my fatigues, tired from being on two hours of sleep the past few days, and freezing from the wind and having to hold my cheek up on top of the metal receiver of my machine gun. When I finished my shift, I wrapped myself and my gear up in a poncho and started thinking about things back in SoCal, and HorseFeather Farm came up. I remembered all the good times we had, and the fun of summer camp and jumping for the first time riding Jumby. And even in those miserable conditions, I still had a huge smile on my face. I can't thank you enough for that. It truly was one of the most fun times of my life.

I am doing all right at USMA. I still miss life back in California, but I've gotten used to it here. I am currently a sophomore (or as we call it, a Yuk), majoring in Russian. I hope to spend a semester next year studying in Ukraine or Kazakhstan. Currently, I am a member of our Aviation team, and I hope to commission as an Aviation officer and be a pilot (1st choice), or as an Armor officer and be a tank platoon leader. Please let me know if you are ever in New York, I would love to give you a tour of West Point!

Remi: Writing this brought tears to my eyes and my heart is full. I met Marcia in August of 2010. My daughter Samantha was five years old, and our family was not sure we would ever find someone who would give lessons to a young child. During a routine visit to Horse Mart, in San Dimas, we had a conversation with an employee named Rhonda. After asking a few questions, she gave us a brochure of instructors and underlined Marcia's name. We gave Marcia a call that day, and the next Saturday,

Samantha had her first riding lesson at Ridge Riders in West Covina, California.

I remember thinking, "Wow, this Marcia person is really nice!" She made us feel welcome, answered all of our horse questions (we had a lot!), and Marcia started Sam on her journey of horse love, and all of the life lessons that come with it.

A few months after we met Marcia, my mother in law, Sam's grandma, suffered from a dissected aorta and underwent a massive surgery. We were told she would not likely survive. She did survive, thank God! But her road to recovery was long and hard. I remember shortly after the surgery, standing by the arena watching Sam ride and just crying. Marcia came beside me and asked if I believed in God (I do), and she stood right there and prayed with me for Sandy. Sandy did make a full recovery, and we are so thankful!

Unfortunately, not long after this, I lost my own mom. As our friendship had grown, Marcia held my hand and walked me through this dark time in my life with her care, and never ceasing prayer for peace and healing. This is where I knew God works in not so mysterious ways. He knew my mom would be leaving this earth so He made sure

I met Marcia who, to this day, is my mentor, my friend, and a major, positive role model for my two daughters.

Fast forward a few years. Marcia and Dick decided to move to Sparks, Nevada, and I am excited for them and their new adventure. I knew it was going to be difficult to be so far away, but at the same time, I was so incredibly grateful that I met her before she left. I know in my heart that if not for Marcia, Sam would not be the passionate and awesome rider she is today and that my own life would be missing an important piece.

Even now, when things get tough, when life throws me a curveball, and I'm at a loss, I call Marcia. She is steadfast in her faith and biblical advice. She finds the humor and helps me navigate through things. A few times a year, we drive past her old house and down to Ridge Riders where we first found Horse Feather Farm. The memories are sweet and deep.

Thank you, Marcia. Thank you for your love and support and for being such an awesome human to every life you have touched.

Emma: "Failure is not falling down but refusing to get back up." What a wonderful idea to write a book about Horse Feather Farm! I can only imagine how many stories you've accumulated from everyone who has been touched by you and your home. I'm sad to hear that the city of West Covina is trying to close down Ridge Riders for good, as so many memories of my childhood are in those arenas.

I'm not even sure where to start when recollecting memories of HFF. Summer 2005 was my first year as a camper with HFF. It was my first real adventure learning how to care for and ride horses! Before that summer, I had only been on trail rides through National Parks. HFF was the foundation for everything I know about horses. After another summer as a camper, I started taking lessons to really develop my riding skills, which eventually led to becoming a camp counselor! As a counselor, I was able to learn how to work with kids and how to teach. I learned how to be more patient because not all kids learn the same; I learned how to better communicate with a wide range of people; I learned how to help solve problems. All of these are lessons I've carried with me to this day! I also constantly remember the yearly inspirational sayings, such as "Humble Winner, Gracious Loser" and "Pay it Forward."

Probably one of my fondest memories of Horse Feather

Farm I have is the last counselor sleepover in fall 2011. Even though we didn't do any riding, it was a night of fun with the family I had made over the last six years. From s'mores in the front driveway to visiting all our favorite trusty steeds, to GiGi's chicken; it was a night to remember for us all!

Another favorite memory is Winner's Circle 2011, and another fun time as a family! I took the most pictures I have ever taken at HFF during this camp for counselors. Although I may not remember every single thing we did, I do remember how much fun we had together. I still love wearing my tie-dye t-shirt, every now and then, as well as many other HFF t-shirts, to showcase my pride for such experiences in my life.

My absolute favorite memory of Horse Feather Farm is all the amazing horses I was able to work with. I'm not even sure I could count how many horses there were, but I do know that Rio, Pepper, Rusty, and Angel will always have a special place in my heart. They taught me so much about who I am and who I want to become. The horses of HFF are the ones who showed me that I wanted to work with horses the rest of my life. They inspired me to follow my dreams and to keep learning everything I could about the equine species.

I am now a college graduate with a major in Equine Science and a minor in Small Business Management. Because of my experiences at Horse Feather Farm, I have had incredible opportunities to further my education with horses. Some of these opportunities include an internship training horses on a ranch in South Dakota, studying Equine Fitness, Equine Anatomy, and English Equitation in Scotland, learning to drive wagons, carts, and hauling logs, working as a stable hand, and training my first horse, who I now own. With so many directions to choose from, I am proud to say that I now work at Circle D Ranch, part of Disneyland Resort. I am able to use the experiences and lessons I've learned from Horse Feather Farm every day at work and with my own horse. Not only do I get to use the horse skills I learned, but I also get to use the people skills and patience I learned as a camp counselor when talking to the guests of Disneyland.

I can't even begin to describe how much Horse Feather Farm has influenced my life. I made lifelong friends, worked with amazing horses, and got to pursue my dreams of working with horses for the rest of my life. There are so many more memories that would take years to tell. I just hope that one day I can touch as many lives as you have.

Liz: I was overjoyed to receive your letter and even more excited to share my thoughts and memories from HFF! I am doing well. I'm now 20 years old, engaged, and working at PetSmart. I stopped riding a year and a half ago from injuries to my spine and tailbone. I miss riding every day, and I hope I can get back at it soon! I've only fallen once in all my years of riding, and I had ridden a retired Kentucky Derby racehorse. He threw me, and I landed back first on a Cavaletti pole and damaged my lumbar spine. I have permanent damage now, but I was lucky not to be paralyzed! You always taught me to get back up, and I did just that. I rode for a year and a half after that and never was afraid.

I still have all my crafts and scrapbooks from all the camps. They were probably the best summers of my life. I often look back at all the memories and wish I could go back in time to relive them. Horse Feather Farm taught me so many life lessons that I use today and in everyday life. It taught me how to respect my coworkers and teammates around me, to work hard, and to love life and enjoy every moment. My favorite memories were after camp we would all go swimming in different people's pools or ride horses around the barn in our swimsuits. There was always so much to do there, and everyone was so friendly and was never judgmental. No one cared what we looked like if we didn't wear makeup because we all came together to ride horses and love animals.

I miss the days when I would wake up first thing in the morning and go to HFF...and have not a care in the world. As an adult, I reminisce about the innocent childhood I had at HFF. It was some of my happiest days and the memories I will never forget. HFF taught me how to catch chickens, how to properly tack horses and, most importantly, how to respect my fellow peers. I always enjoyed doing the crafts and tie-dying our T-shirts. I'll never forget when I pranked a kid by putting wasabi on a sushi roll and watched him turn purple, or when I got hosed in the face by the counselors. I always had so much fun, and I wish so badly that we could all reunite and have a reunion and see where everyone else is in life. I'll never forget how great HFF was to me. Every memory from HFF is so precious, and I hope I never forget them or forget the people that share those memories with me. I'd like to say thank you to all that made horse camp possible because that was the best time of my life and I'll never forget how much it helped prepare you for the real life, and to never stop loving animals.

Kimmy: I have so many fond memories of my time at Horse Feather Farm. Some of my favorites are Golden Bowl runs, bringing the farm to Sonrise Christian School, blackberry picking while also trying to avoid being bit by the crawfish, counselor sleepovers, dancing to the Cha Cha Slide in the living room, finger-painting the horses during camp, watching the Saddle Club movies, the ice cream sundae I never earned (because I never fell off a horse), bunny races around the barn (which may or may not have caused us to have more bunnies), and Rambo and all the other animals on the farm throughout the years.

Marcia always made us feel like we were her own children, and I will forever be thankful for her influence in my life. I learned so much about horses, myself, and leadership. I learned how to be a good leader, how to work with all different kinds of people from all different backgrounds, and how to be a good teacher/trainer and to be patient with people that do not learn in the same way that I do.

Since HFF I have gone to school for Hospitality Management with an emphasis in Event Management. I got married to my high school sweetheart in 2013. We then moved to Arizona for him to continue his schooling to become a pastor. I am now working for Enliven Production Group which produces large corporate events all over the country.

Cadence: Here is my short attempt to capture the most important memories and lessons from my time at Horse Feather Farm. There are too many things to list, but I think I got my favorite ones :) I got emotional writing this as I am so nostalgic about those wonderful summers at the farm and so grateful for all you gave to us horse crazy kids!

I am writing this from my hotel room in Coachella Valley - I am showing at Thermal for two weeks! Wouldn't be here without you!

Growing up spending time at Horse Feather Farm and Ridge Riders shaped my childhood. I cannot imagine my life without Marcia, the animals, and friends I made there. Not only was I able to cultivate my love of horses under Marcia's watchful eye, but I was also allowed just to be a kid in such a wholesome, freeing way that few city slickers get to experience these days.

Although my riding lessons and horse shows were probably the most important to me when I was young, my fondest memories looking back are actually of days at

"Farm Camp." Besides being a bit more laid back than it's horse-focused counterpart, Farm Camp was when we got to play with all the animals that lived at the farm, make applesauce, pick berries at the creek, play games (Aunt Mary's Kitchen!!), build miniature farms, and more. To me, those fun-filled days really captured what summer was supposed to be like. I feel so incredibly lucky to have such pure memories of those simple times.

Having joined the HFF family at seven years old, I spent many summers going to camp as both a camper and a counselor. But my favorite year by far was the last. It was the summer before my senior year, and since I knew it was the last chance I'd get, I decided to work as many camps as I could, and I am so glad that I did. Every day was truly a joy, spent with wonderful kids and counselors alike under the California sun, sharing the gift of horses. It really doesn't get better than that. Best of all, I got to share it with my siblings. My sister Allegra worked as a counselor beside me, and we even somehow convinced our brother to attend horse camp.

I'll never forget that on "demonstration day," when the campers perform a pattern to show off their new riding skills, Pepper "ran away" with Daj mid-ride. By running away, I mean slowly cantering across the arena as Daj unknowingly encouraged her by leaning forward while trying to pull her back. Everyone was shouting directions at him in between giggles. I don't think he has been on a horse since!

Looking back, I feel like that unforgettable summer was my childhood coming to a close. It was a perfect way to spend my last summer before I had to worry about college, work, and all the fun things that come with being a young adult. Those golden days will be with me always.

I could talk about fun times at camp or memorable moments on horseback forever. Along with all I have to look back on, I also learned so much from Marcia and my time with the HFF team. So many of our little mottos like, "Humble Winner, Gracious Loser" or "Leave a place better than you found it," have stuck with me throughout the years. They pop back into my head when I need them, and sometimes I even catch myself saying them to others. It's pretty amazing how these simple life lessons can become a part of your personal culture.

Besides the more literal life lessons she taught me, Marcia led by example and showed me the importance of acceptance and understanding. She created a safe haven for all types of young people from all walks of life. No matter the person's story or circumstance, they were welcome at the farm and in her home. We were always to treat each other with respect, love, and empathy. It showed me how important it was to be open to others, despite first impressions or differences.

I can't forget to mention my other teacher, my beloved Angel. My early riding days with her as my partner set the foundation for the rest of my Equestrian career to date. Not only did she make me a better rider, but she taught me the value of hard work and patience. The foundation of safe, responsible horsemanship from Marcia and fiery little Angel allowed my passion to flourish as well as set me up for a successful future. I didn't grow up riding at the fanciest barn on an expensive horse, but I wouldn't have it any other way. I didn't get to show on the A circuit, but I got to barrel race, jump bareback, and trail ride in the creek. I even got to bring Angel to school for show and tell in fifth grade (my classmates still remember this and bring it up to me - seriously!). For a little horse crazy girl, it was a magical childhood and one I wouldn't trade for anything. Thank you, Marcia - I love you!

Hanah: Where and how do I even begin to sum up my memories and lessons learned from Horse Feather Farm? Looking back, I have realized that I learned a ton of life skills, thanks to one particularly beautiful, yet opinionated mare named Sparkle. The next little bit is going to be in bullet style of the things I learned...

1. I learned patience... learning that "good things come to those who wait," and I learned to put a solid foundation down so I could have something to build on down the line, but to be patient enough to know that "down the line" could take awhile to get to.

2. I learned respect... If Sparkle thought you were even remotely trying to boss her around or correct her unfairly, you found out very quickly. I learned that trust and respect are things that are built slowly, which goes back to the patience, and that if you rush, you can undo your work in a fraction of the time it took to earn.

3. I learned trust... I will admit there were days I went to mount Sparkle for a riding lesson and right off the bat I knew this was going to be an interesting ride, especially when I first started riding her. After a bit of time and showing her that I was going to be fair, but at the same time she had to be fair with me, our relationship blossomed. However, had I gotten on the first time and had a hard hand/leg and used spurs and a crop/whip out of line, simply because I had not learned how to use them correctly, and/or did not have

the muscle capacity to do more than one thing at a time, it would have taken a ton more time just rebuilding that trust that I broke right off the bat.

4. I learned responsibility... I learned that you always put your animals needs first. Even if you got done with a lesson or a ride in general and were beyond exhausted and super sore, the horse still got taken care of first… and no cutting corners there either. I learned that even if someone isn't watching or doesn't specifically tell you to do something you feel needs to be done, you do it. A little lesson called "Integrity."

But most of all what I learned was to love. To love those who might not be perfect, or might just not understand you, but to love each person/animal for who they are only expecting the best they can give, not comparing their best to anyone else's.

Sam: I remember my very first lesson with Marcia at Horse Feather Farm. It was on Charlie, and he was one sassy pony I will never forget!

I rode Charlie for a while and then moved on to Pepper, or as I called her, "Pepper Love". She was the most kind-hearted, sweet mare ever. Boy did she teach me a lot, from two-pointing (an exercise on a horse), to going on trail rides, to not giving up when it got hard. Our first show together was the best! We won all of our three lead line classes. That was when I learned to be a "gracious winner, humble loser". Pepper Love will have a special place in my heart for the rest of my life.

Another one of my favorite memories was horse camp. We went to the home of the Forgettes and made "horsey handprints" while singing silly songs. Marcia made everything about horse camp special.

Marcia has been and continues to be a huge presence in my life. She gives wise advice, she's funny, and I would not be where I am today if Marcia had never crossed my path. Thank you, Marcia, for all of the knowledge you have bestowed upon me.

Bonnie: Well, as far as memories of Horse Feather Farm go, I just have so many, and all of them are so fond. I'd like to start by saying that I had always admired you and your patience with all of us kids! You were like a second mother to me all those years of growing up.

I remember the camaraderie amongst us kids, we all really became a family. And it's the little things that make me smile when I think about them, like going up to the top area of the property to gather duck eggs, or mucking the stalls- Yes, I remember looking forward to mucking. I never saw it as a chore. I saw it as a few more minutes spent with the horses I loved so dearly. Memories of Rambo spring to mind and us girls trying to essentially ride him. Poor thing.

I used to love riding down to the creek to find crawdads and blackberries that Dale would then cook up for us during camp. And speaking of camp, I just remember those little kids, the girls especially, looking up to us older girls so much and hanging on to every word we said. Being a camp counselor taught me a lot about how I presented myself, knowing the younger girls were looking up to all of us. And it gave me a sense of pride knowing I was helping to teach the children little life lessons here and there. I laugh when I think about our large sleepover and all us girls tee-peeing Scott's room when he was away!

As for me now, I still have Apache down at my parent's house and ride him every time I'm down. He and I rode in the Extreme Cowboy Association races, and we won the year-end high point belt buckle! I gave riding lessons on him for several years and felt that being a camp counselor at HFF really helped me learn how to teach and convey my thoughts properly to my students.

We currently live in the Bay Area and love being up here. I'm a photographer and also work for a dog walking and pet sitting company during the week just for fun and some extra cash. David and I love to travel and have lived in several different cities since we've been married (10 years next May!). We hope to have a large country property with horses and various farm animals someday. But in the meantime, we're happy with our semi-nomadic lives and loving our pets. No babies over here though. Kitties are hard enough to get a sitter for when we travel.

I'm really excited to see all the other memories of my old friends. Take care, Marcia, much love!!

Robin: My family's path to meet Marcia Cromie started when I, in my minivan with three children under the age of seven, followed a miniature horse tied to a golf cart entering Ridge Riders on Citrus Avenue. That minivan would stop on a dime if there was a horse in sight. My kids loved animals, and to say that my daughters loved horses was more than an understatement. I'm often asked where the girls got their love of horses, and I could never explain it. My oldest came out of the womb with this passion.

So, we followed that golf cart, asked the man driving it if anyone gave riding lessons there, and met Marcia just days later at the arena where she was simultaneously giving a lesson and hosting a casual potluck.

Typical Marcia, doing three things at once and seemingly effortlessly, making everyone feel warm and welcome in the process. On that day lifelong friendships were born, and we discovered a treasured place where we would spend countless hours, just a couple of miles from home.

Marcia, Dick, and HFF taught more lessons than we can recall or adequately describe in words. Coming from rural towns in the Midwest, we were thrilled that our kids found a little bit of country and a hard-working, compassionate sensibility that will stay with them for their lifetimes. Though our son didn't ride, Ridge Riders and HFF were places he could get dirty, learn to respect and care for animals, and play among diverse kids and be sensitive to the strengths and struggles of others. Marcia and Dick were amazing role models to our kids which was especially touching to us since we had no family in California at the time. HFF was a second home to them, a place where they felt safe, loved and challenged to be better human beings.

Our girls learned so much from Marcia and her ever-changing herd of lesson horses. The horses were as diverse as the kids that rode them, each with their own story and none a perfect specimen in or outside the arena. Our girls learned to work hard, not just on themselves and their riding ability, but to care for the horses and, over time, earn their trust and affection that was necessary in the arena. They learned what kids learn from being an athlete regarding practicing, listening to a coach, managing their time, discipline, and work ethic. Perhaps most importantly, they learned that their "sport" depended on another living being, a 1,000-pound living being, that is subject to emotion, fatigue, hunger, pain, joy, fear, pride, and misunderstanding. As their abilities and experience grew, so did their confidence on and off the horse.

As sisters close in age and experience, our girls had an added challenge of competing in the same events. Though we always taught them they were in the arena to be the best they could be rather than be better than others; there was still the potential for jealousy and resentment. We honestly never saw any negative emotions or behavior. We saw our girls, along with the others representing HFF, support each other deeply as each of them excelled or struggled. They learned that no matter how skilled and prepared, everyone, and every horse, will have good days and bad days. Feeling everyone's triumph and pain brought lots of emotion but taught them about compassion and the supportive power a caring culture provides. Their character grew not from what happened in the arena, but how they responded to it. They learned to care for a community of people and the importance of being there for others.

These are just a few of the life lessons the Cromie's and HFF brought to our family. We are incredibly grateful for Marcia and Dick as role models and now, family.

Erin N: I would like to thank you for the ten years of wonderful memories, lessons and opportunities you have given me. I've been so blessed for finding this place a becoming a part of it. From mucking the stalls to roasting marshmallows, I've loved it all! I especially loved washing the pigs, jumping, and meeting all my friends. The camps were such a life-changing experience. I'm proud to say I horseback ride with Horse Feather Farm. This was one of the places that made me who I am. Marcia, you have shaped me into the lady I am today. You are such a compassionate and unique woman; very amiable and patient. I never thought this day would come but I hope you enjoy Nevada. You deserve a break! It's hard to say goodbye to you and the horses, goats and especially pigs. Don't worry; I suspect all of us counselors will get together again soon. Even with this chapter of our lives closing, we will always keep it in our hearts and minds. Thank you for everything! P.S. If the person taking the pigs ever wants someone to come over and wash them or brush them, let them know they can call me!

Halee: How I first met Marcia: It was a Friday and my mom had just picked my brother and I (10 years old) from school. Instead of driving straight home for some reason that day, my mom took us around some parts of Covina. She then turned into a baseball field and noticed there was a hidden area in the back of the fields and we came across Ridge Riders Horse Equestrian Arenas. We all got out of the car and walked up to a tall, loud blonde lady that was yelling directions to a student riding a horse. Little did I realize that lady, Marcia Cromie would change my life.

Once my mom and Marcia were done talking about horseback riding lessons that Marcia offered, my mom asked me if I wanted to do gymnastics or start riding lessons. Of course, the choice I made that day was one of the best decisions I have ever made.

When I first started riding lessons, my mom took my

brother Everton, his friend Max, my friend Connie and me, and we all took lessons together for a while. The more I took lessons and got closer to Marcia, she invited me to her house to start loading horses and start saddling them to get them prepared for each of her lessons, as well as finishing everything up, loading the horses for back home and preparing food to feed all of her animals. It was such an amazing experience, and it taught me how much it took taking care of an animals of all kind. She didn't just have horses, she had bunnies, goats, sheep, chickens, a rooster, ducks, pigs, dogs and a cat. Not long after, I decided I was going to become a vegetarian. I loved animals so much that, in my mind, I thought I could never raise any animal like the happy animals on her farm and eat it. Since that day, I still am a vegetarian at the age of 26.

There were so many memories growing up: Going to church with her and her family, meeting best friends that had the same passions for horses like I do, staying overnight at her house with my friends, setting up our alarms to see the horses laying down sleeping, being a counselor at her Horse Feather Farm Camps, going swimming after camps at the neighbor's pool, dancing to the "Cha Cha Slide", traveling around to compete in Horse Shows and playing fun games during the play days. I think I've helped with every position there was at events at Ridge Riders. I handed out ribbons, I opened and closed the gates before and after every category, I helped in the kitchen, helped the announcer and helped with registration. The true meaning of "work hard, play hard."

Not only was Marcia a big part of my memories, but her family was too. I got to know her husband Dick, and her youngest son Scott very well, both were always entertaining. From Dick's hilarious Christmas cards and Scott's daily stories. Scott also taught my friend Katie and I a word of the day. The last word he taught that I remember was "indelibly." I also got to meet her mother, sisters, nieces etc. She always made me feel like I was a part of the family.

Later in my teenage years when my family moved away, I bought a horse of my own and still Marcia was always there to help me and give me advice.

I can honestly say Marcia was a big influence on the person I am today. Not only did she teach me almost everything I know about animals, she taught me good morals and values that I use in life. Kindness, hard work, love, friend, family and forgiveness are only a few examples.

The woman I am today, a young, smart, beautiful hotel

manager taking over Las Vegas, one hotel at a time, and I can thank her for helping raise me. As she always said, "It takes a village."

Madison: Horse Feather Farm truly defined my life for so many years. I learned the greatest lessons in patience, friendship, and responsibility through my relationships to the horses and people that HFF, and more specifically, Marcia introduced me to.

Camps were much more than any other. The complete immersion into the world of a horse owner (the good, the bad, and the dirty) provided an understanding and appreciation for ownership and the craft of riding rather than simply learning to ride. I believe the holistic style of Horsey Camp inspired more intuitive riders, and by extension students of the world. The frustrations on horseback with more challenging horsey companions has instilled a greater sense of determination and patience in me today. The coaching from Marcia to take a few deep breaths, count backwards, and find my calm during particularly difficult rides atop Sparkle or Angel are skills that I still employ, whether it's a challenging academic, professional, or interpersonal situation. My time as a counselor deepened my understanding for the mission of HFF and Horsey

Camp. Through supervision and instruction, I was able to solidify my own understanding of the tasks at hand, and find my passion for working with others.

Since my time at HFF, I have gone on to study Environmental Policy and become civically engaged. My passion to educate others and work to create positive change stems from the camp themes and practice. The words most important to me when I'm asked about character or relationships are directly pulled from the annual theme and discussion around cornerstone characteristics, such as integrity. I miss you! Love from our family!

Linda: What Horse Feather Farm Has Meant To Me and My Family:

Like all mothers we want all of our children's dreams to come true – yes even the dreams that include horses. When my twins were about seven years old I set out on a quest to help them realize all of their horsey dreams. Little did I know that finding Horse Feather Farm would alter my children's lives in a very positive way.

My twins started Farm Camp when they were seven years old and we never looked back. They learned how to care for farm animals and eventually care, love, and nurture horses. We have helped stitch up horses, clean duck ponds, feed chickens, pet pigs' bellies, run from aggressive goats, and yes pick up more horse poop than I care to remember. We have accomplished all of these things rain or shine; good mood or bad mood, when money was tight, and when times were stressful. My children have learned how to empathize, teach, and love via animals, children, and adults whom they interacted with while working and playing. My husband and I couldn't be more grateful for our children's time at Horse Feather Farm.

My children are now adults and they both actively live that experience on a daily basis. One of my children is an Animal Control Officer and the other is studying to be a veterinarian – so thank you, Marcia and Dick, for helping us raise our children!

Oh – and I did have a few years where I helped Marcia with Summer Camps! Life moves forward but there are some days where I miss the shenanigans!

Allegra: Horse Feather Farm was everything an animal-loving child could dream of growing up around. I was fortunate enough to have found the HFF family and spent so much time with the people and animals that made it so incredible. I wasn't always aware of the life lessons I was learning and the values I was developing during my time there. Looking back, I can see how much my experiences at HFF influenced the person I have become. The environment the Cromies created taught me independence and appreciation for all forms of life.

Marcia created an environment that allowed me to grow and develop independence. Marcia was there to guide and teach me. Just as important, she granted me the freedom to do things on my own when she believed I could. I was given leadership responsibilities at a younger age than most, as a junior camp counselor. She never let my age determine my abilities to take on a new challenge. I believe this dynamic to Marcia's teaching style helped me develop confidence and independence.

HFF really instilled the importance of acceptance into me. Acceptance, appreciation and love for others – both humans and animals alike. Being surrounded by these values taught me that people's differences are what make them unique and beautiful. In camp, we were always taught to have patience, compassion and love for others. There was no tolerance for conflict, and these sort of situations hardly ever took place.

I cannot imagine my childhood without Horse Feather Farm. It makes up so many fond memories spent with my siblings, and (both human and animal) friends. I can remember making the sneaky venture out in the dark and chilly night to see the horses sleeping so clearly, or taking the golf cart to chase after Freckles on one of her infamous "Great Escapes", or hearing Marcia's expected reminder to "keep your Mables off the table..." (Mable, Mable, if you're able, get your elbows off the table; this is not a horse's stable!), as we gather around the table for a serving of the glorious "Gigi's chicken."

I hold the pure memories I have at Ridge Riders and Horse Feather farm so close to my heart. I was encouraged to be myself and got to spend my childhood surrounded by nature, in a safe environment with loving people and beautiful animals. My experiences and time spent there shaped me into the person I am today, and I will forever be grateful for that.

Jessica: Marcia, you have made such a huge impact on my life. During my hard times, all I wanted to do was to get back into riding and push everything else behind me, and there was no other place I would have rather gone than to Horse Feather Farm. I am so very fortunate that you opened up your home and heart, and allowed for me to become part a of your family. I could never have imagined myself showing and being as successful as I am if it were not for you and all your hard work. Thank you so much. I am so very grateful! My love always...

Katie: I just want to thank you, Marcia for all the wonderful things you have done for me...for all the life lessons, for the gifts, and for the love. You have always been like a second mom to me and I have appreciated that very much throughout my life. I know I wasn't always the easiest person to get along with and I thank you for your understanding all those times I yelled at you. I also want to thank you for the many times you have pushed me to my limits when I didn't want to. I love you with all my heart!

Raina: (Michael's #2 daughter): I remember some summers going up to L.A; my parents would drop my sister Sam and me off to our Nana who had a horse camp up there. I remember I had a favorite horse that was named Charley and I pretended he was mine.

There were times when our leaders would have us do a bunch of activities, and they would give us stars on our tags. Later I found out they were giving us these ribbons and small trophies. Looking back at it, the camp leaders made sure each of the students felt special giving each of us a reward and ribbons, even participation award just so we didn't feel left out, which looking back on was the funniest thing ever.

When camp was over at the end of the day, I just remember sometimes going up to the farm by myself at night and just think and look at the night, at the same time being aware that Rambo, the rude goat, wasn't near me... that is a whole other story.

Samantha: (Michael's #1 daughter): I think my very first year of horse camp was when I was about to turn nine. Since that first year, my little sister Raina and I would go down to So Cal every summer and spend a week with Nana and Papa. My Nana was the director of the horse camp so it was always a fun thing to do with her every summer till I turned 12. So, for three years I attended horse camp.

I would say one of my favorite memories was making new friends every year and having sleepovers with them. Horse camp really helped me socialize with other kids my age and by the end of the week, I shared some close friendships.

Another memory that I cherished was waking up early before camp and being able to help feed the horses and groom them with Nana. I remember riding in the golf cart up to the barn and helping Nana getting the hay, or mixing in vitamins in the horses' food. Nana's junior counselors would also come in the morning, and then all of us would clean and organize and load the horses into the trailer.

During the week, on occasion, we would also go up to the barn after camp, and then climb through the stables to get to the neighbor's backyard so that we could take care of their horses. I don't know why, but I really enjoyed that part of my summer vacation. I just really loved being close to the horses and taking responsibility for them with Nana.

Nana also taught a moral lesson of the week too, like the theme for camp that we would always try to apply outside of camp, which was a really cool thing.

Marisa: A lot has changed since I saw you last. I am a mother to the most handsome baby boy named Ananiah (from the Book of Nehamiah), which means protected by God. In 2017, I graduated with my bachelor's in psychology from Cal State Los Angeles University, and that summer I married my best friend and the father of my son. It is only through prayers and God's blessings, His provisions, grace and favor that we are all together today. And I am so excited to share my memories of Horse Feather Farm with you.

I spend so much time telling my husband and son amazing stories about Kali. I tell them what an amazing blessing she was to me at the time and I loved her so much. To this day, I wish I still had her because I know my son would have fallen in love with her, too. Kali gave me such a great experience, and one day I hope to give my son the same experience. I want to have my own horse again just so Ananiah can feel and see how it is to own a horse. Those were really some of the greatest days of my life. Kali was so fun and she brought so much joy into my life. Having her for four years was wonderful for me because she helped me to cope through my father's illness. After hard days of chemotherapy with him, I would come home and go out into the backyard and spend time with her. But it was in the midst of times like this that brought us closer. I never thanked you enough for allowing this incredible animal to stay at my house; I was happiest when she was by my side.

So thank you, Marcia, for allowing me to love her and for allowing her to make me smile and laugh even through my tears. I wish you and your family the very best. I could not have asked for a better horse to be my first. Much love, always.

Some Favorite Themes From Campers & Counselors

Galen: "Humble Winner, Gracious Loser"—This theme taught me that winning isn't everything. It also taught me that when you win, you shouldn't be bragging. Also that it's okay to lose and you should be thankful to have the opportunity to be in the competition.

Emma: "Humble Winner, Gracious Loser" "Pay It Forward"—The things I take with me forever are all the lessons I've learned like having more patience, all my riding skills, treating others with more respect than I could imagine. I'll also take with me all the great memories of HFF that have shaped me as a person in the seven years I've been here. It's an end of an era, an end to my childhood and an end to everything I've grown up with. In the end, everything will go on with me, the memories of the horses and all my new friends; Marcia, Dick, Linda, Erin and even

Jimmy. There isn't a way that I could not take the memory of everyone and everything with me into my future. I hope to pass on everything I've learned to those I meet and the children I may have one day.

Taylor: "Honesty is the Best Policy"—I learn integrity, work ethic and how to face my fears. I learned that honesty is the best policy and that God is sovereign over all I do, even around the horses! I learned how precious friends are and how blessed I am to have a place like Horsey Camp to enjoy horses and have fun with them. Thank you Marcia, Dick, Erin and Jimmy for giving me this opportunity. I will always remember it!

Jason: "Pay it Forward"—This theme I like the most because if we didn't pay it forward, we wouldn't be here learning about horses!

Bethany: "Caring is Sharing" "Going the Extra Mile" & "Leave a Place Better Than You Found It"—I will take with me my memories and all the fun times with Marcia and the kids, the counselors and the horses and that caring for others is one of the best gifts you can give.

Julianna: "Pay it Forward"—One of my biggest most vivid memories with HFF was the day I first cantered at HFF. I was just getting off Friday and Marcia told me I was a good rider. I had been riding for three years and that was the first and only time anyone ever told me I was good. One thing I have learned and will take with me is when Marcia taught me to believe in myself. Because of her, I believe I can do much more than I did. Thank you, Marcia!

Alyssa: "Pay It Forward"—This theme is special to me because I think that everyone should pay it forward and do things like what Marcia has done for us.

Cadence: "Something You can Take Away"—Be accountable. This theme stuck out the most to me. It's all about commitment, dedication and responsibility. Being accountable for yourself and your actions is so valuable in being a mature respectful person. Taking responsibility for your own mistakes is especially difficult and courageous. The most memorable thing about HFF for me is the welcoming home and family that has always been here for me. Being able to be comfortable and be myself was so important as I was growing up. It made me more confident in myself, and I know it changed me as a person.

John G: "Be Accountable"—Own up to what you do. Always take responsibility for everything you do.

Erin: "Attitude of Gratitude"—This theme has stuck with me to be thankful for everything and everyone, and not only in thanksgiving. I say thanks all the time because I have found to believe that no good deed should go unnoticed. So thank you, Marcia!

Unknown: "Pay It Forward"—Here at HFF, I have learned to be a better person and not to take life for granted. This life has so much to give and we need to take it and share it with others, so that they can have a chance at the same happiness that you had!

Unknown: "Leave a Place Better Than You Found it"—Leave a person or place better than you found them. I can be myself and I shouldn't worry about what others think about me.

Through The Years

"But ask the animals, and they will teach you,
or the birds in the sky, and they will tell you;
In his hand is the life of every creature
and the breath of all mankind." (Job 12:7,10)

Our Victorian home in Andover, Massachusetts - 1964

My Family at Easter 1967 (L to R)
Nancy with Queenie, Georgia, Mollie,
Mom (Mary), Me, Dad (Lou) and Ringo

"Tous Ensemble"- Jenny & Me - 1966

Mr. Chester "Chet" Abbott with Monohogany

Mr. Abbott's house

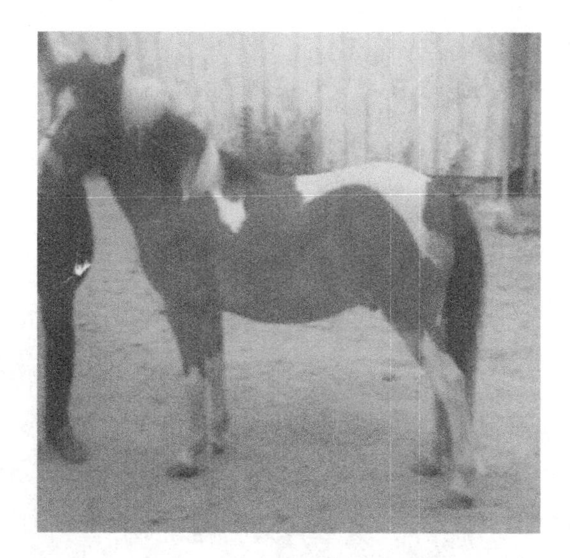

Friskie

Me & Patches in front of my house -1965

Me & Monohogany at local show circa - 1964

Me & Napoleon...rented horse, borrowed clothes!
At North Andover Riding Academy Horseshow 1965

My Wedding Party April 14, 1973
Bloomington, Indiana

Dick & I escaping in our new car!

Aerial view of Horse Feather Farm
Covina, CA - 2010

Me & Knothead when I first bought him at
Foster's TJ Quarter Horse Ranch

Craft Time

Camp Van & 4 (and a half) Horse Trailer

Me & a young Rambo at Ridge Riders

Linda & Bentley

Bonnie & Abby at Ridge Riders

Cisneros' Grandpa Ron with baby George

L to R: Heather & Sparkle, Cadence & Angel
Katie & Jumby at horse show
Sycamore Cyn Stables

La Verne, California 4th of July Parade
Katie & Rusty - Me & Kali

Bentley bucking - Anna riding - Jess staring

Blackberry picking in Walnut Creek

Farm Camp

Jack demonstrating how to shoe a horse for my class at Sonrise Christian School

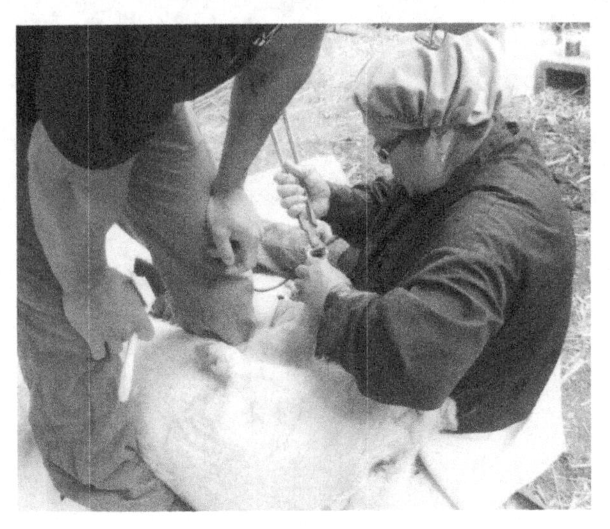

Kelly the "Pig Lady" trimming George's hooves

Horse Camp

Rusty surprising Sam on her birthday

Nana with Izzy on Friday

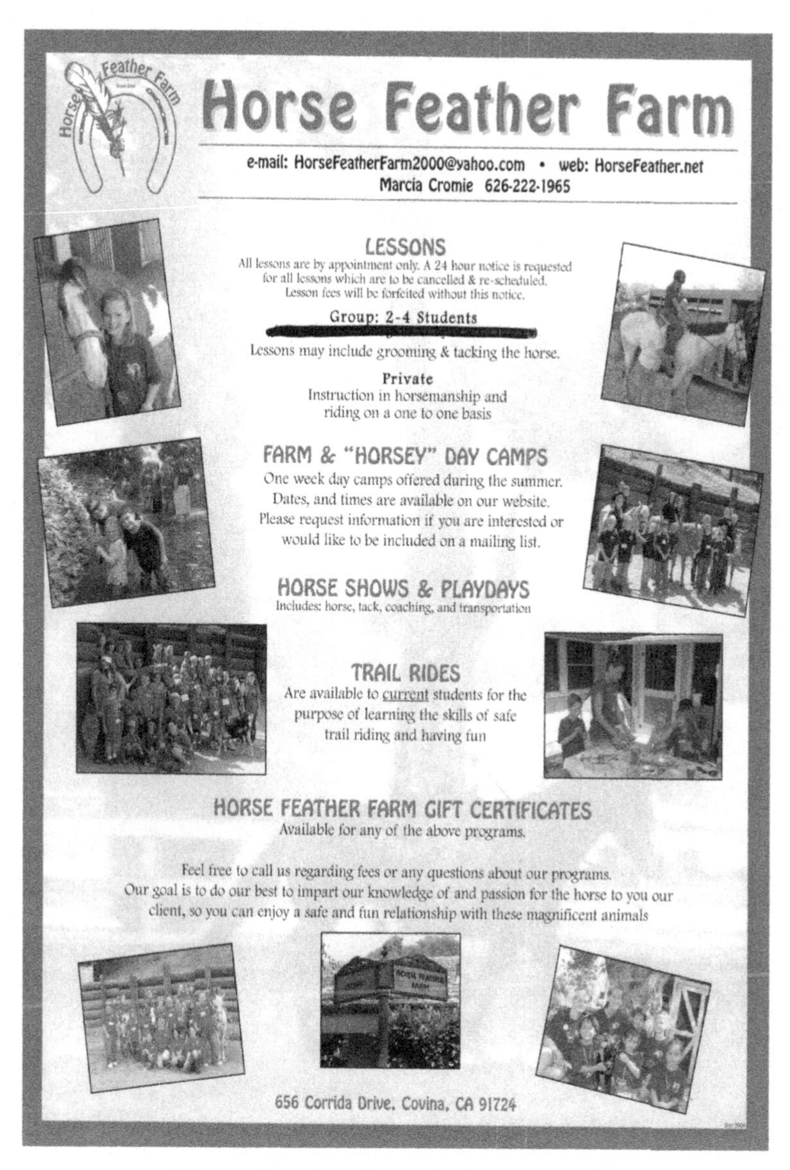

Horse Feather Farm

e-mail: HorseFeatherFarm2000@yahoo.com • web: HorseFeather.net
Marcia Cromie 626-222-1965

LESSONS

All lessons are by appointment only. A 24 hour notice is requested for all lessons which are to be cancelled & re-scheduled. Lesson fees will be forfeited without this notice.

Group: 2-4 Students

Lessons may include grooming & tacking the horse.

Private

Instruction in horsemanship and riding on a one to one basis

FARM & "HORSEY" DAY CAMPS

One week day camps offered during the summer. Dates, and times are available on our website. Please request information if you are interested or would like to be included on a mailing list.

HORSE SHOWS & PLAYDAYS

Includes: horse, tack, coaching, and transportation

TRAIL RIDES

Are available to current students for the purpose of learning the skills of safe trail riding and having fun

HORSE FEATHER FARM GIFT CERTIFICATES

Available for any of the above programs.

Feel free to call us regarding fees or any questions about our programs.
Our goal is to do our best to impart our knowledge of and passion for the horse to you our client, so you can enjoy a safe and fun relationship with these magnificent animals

656 Corrida Drive, Covina, CA 91724

Horse Feather Farm Information Flyer